a Layman Looks at the Lord's prayer

W. Phillip Keller

a Layman Looks at the Lord's prayer

W. Phillip Keller

MOODY PRESS
CHICAGO

© 1976 by
THE MOODY BIBLE INSTITUTE
OF CHICAGO
All rights reserved

Fifth Printing, 1977

Library of Congress Cataloging in Publication Data
Keller, Weldon Philip, 1920—
    A layman looks at the Lord's prayer.

    1. Lord's prayer. 1. Title.
BV230.K36   226'.96'077   75-31635

ISBN 0-8024-4644-2

Printed in the United States of America

In honor of my father,
a
humble layman
who
walked with God.

Acknowledgments

A word of gratitude is due those many men and women who, across the years, have sat in my Bible studies, absorbing truths contained in this work. Had it not been for those willing to study God's Word with me, there would not have been the delightful incentive to search deeply for the great meanings implied in the Lord's Prayer.

Also, my genuine appreciation is extended to my wife, who, with great care and affection, typed and prepared the final manuscript for publication. Often we have prayed together that this book be used widely by God our Father to inspire and encourage His children the world over.

Contents

THE LORD'S PRAYER

9 Our Father which art in heaven, Hallowed be thy name.

10 Thy kingdom come. Thy will be done in earth, as it is in heaven.

11 Give us this day our daily bread.

12 And forgive us our debts, as we forgive our debtors.

13 And lead us not into temptation, but deliver us from evil: For thine is the kingdom, and the power, and the glory, for ever. Amen.

MATTHEW 6:9-13

Preface

Next to Psalm 23, perhaps the most beloved and certainly the best-known passage in Scripture is the Lord's Prayer. It has been repeated millions upon millions of times by countless numbers of human beings for nearly twenty centuries. Yet, in spite of so much use, in spite of so much repetition, in spite of so much worldwide familiarity, it has never lost its luster.

The profound, eternal concepts compressed into its few, concise phrases shine with enduring brilliance. These truths radiated from the very heart of our Lord as He moved among men. They embrace the deepest secrets of God, quietly stated in human language of disarming simplicity. Some of the petitions included in this prayer by Christ were utterly revolutionary. If fully grasped by us, they can overturn much of our own wrong thinking about God.

The Lord's Prayer, in the King James version, contains only sixty-six words. It can be repeated in less than a minute. Despite its brevity, it has been an enormous benefit to multitudes of men and women. Many of them knew little or nothing else about the Scriptures. Yet there is inherent in this prayer all the strength and compassion of our Father in heaven. There moves through it a beauty and serenity which no mortal man can fully explain. It reassures our hearts, strengthens our resolve, and leads us into personal contact with God, our Father.

Much that is deep and profound has already been written about this prayer. Still, that does not dissuade me from writing about it as a layman. To me it is a most precious passage. And here, as in my previous book, *A Shepherd Looks at Psalm 23,* I dare to share with the reader what these Scriptures mean to me—an ordinary man and a child of God.

ONE

Our Father

"Our Father."

What an intimate, personal, family-like approach to God. What a reassuring, comfortable way in which to address the Almighty, Creator of heaven and earth. Can it be that He, who is from everlasting to everlasting, the infinite One, really regards me as His child? Does He care enough to consider me His own son?

This is a startling concept.

It is unique. It stands as a brand new revelation of God, given to us with repeated emphasis and clarity by Christ.

Prior to the time of Jesus, God was regarded as someone remote and august in His demeanor. He sat in the high and holy place, a stern Judge behind the hard, harsh bar of the Law. Only with fear and foreboding did any man dare to address himself to such a powerful potentate.

All through the Old Testament account of God's dealing with His people He is referred to as YAHWEH, the name which dared not be spoken for fear of offense. Fewer than seven times is He even referred to as a father, except indirectly and rather remotely.

Yet in the first four gospels, Jesus, the Christ, casting aside all restraint, speaks of God as Father more than seventy times. It is a radical, new, and very exciting disclosure that God is our Father. Suddenly it puts man's relationship to Him into an entirely new light. He moves from behind the bar of justice to come knocking on the door of our human hearts. He enters our lives to become a "Father to the fatherless."

The whole concept is replete with wonder and incredible love. It hardly seems possible that He who has been from everlasting to everlasting, the eternal, infinite God, should delight to have us call Him, "Our Father."

But not all of us can do this either easily or in sincerity. It is a frightening fact that for many people, the word *father* does not denote a dear one. It does not conjure up the thought of a happy home. Rather, to them it may well be a repulsive and abhorrent title.

Many people have known only harsh, hard fathers. Their human father may have been a selfish, self-centered person who cared little for their well-being. He may have been a derelict, a drunkard, a dope addict, or some other distorted person who wrought havoc with their personalities in early childhood.

Or the human father may have been a weak-willed person who could command no respect from his children. He may have neglected his duties to his home and family, so that he earned only contempt and scorn from his offspring. Even at his very best, he may have at times fluctuated in his moods and temper, one day lenient in dealing with his children, the next tough and terrifying. So how could one so inconsistent, so unpredictable, be trusted?

Little do many fathers know the importance of their role in shaping the characters of their children at an

early age. Long before boys and girls are even off to
school, the cast of their characters and the pattern of
their personalities have been shaped under the parents'
hands in the home. More often than we would admit,
this is a period of pain to the child. Deep doubts and
miserable misgivings arise in the malleable minds of
youngsters. They wonder if they are really wanted. They
long to know if they are really loved. They search for
someone who can really be trusted, someone who really
understands them.

Because of all this the name *father,* instead of being
rich with warm and happy memories, is frequently associated with fear and repulsion, anger and hostility,
sometimes even hate and scorn.

And the tragedy is that in ascribing the title to God as
our Father, we sometimes unconsciously transfer to
Him all those debasing attributes associated in our
minds with our human fathers.

Of course this is not done deliberately. Still, it is done.
The consequences for both us and God can be devastating. We do Him an enormous injustice by superimpos-
ing upon His character the facsimile of a human father.
At very best it can be no more than a caricature, a
distortion of His true being.

If our human fathers have been fair, honest, decent
individuals, then our mental picture of God is bound to
be more favorable. If they have been generous, loving,
gentle men, endowed with more than the usual degree
of human understanding and compassion, this will en-
hance our concept of what God may be like. And it is
inevitable that, in our minds, we will take a more magnanimous view of God.

But the fact remains that, to a large degree, our
thoughts and ideas of God as our Father are conditioned

by our childhood impressions and recollections of our rather frail and fallible human fathers. Far, far too often we ascribe to God in heaven all the weaknesses, idiosyncrasies, failings, and inconsistencies of our very unpredictable human fathers.

None of this was in the mind of Christ when He spoke so sincerely and so simply of God as His Father. His view of God was not conditioned by His childhood relationship to Joseph, the carpenter of Nazareth, but by His own personal identity with God the Father throughout the eons of eternity.

He alone knew fully the true essence of God's character. He alone comprehended the beauty and integrity and wonder of God's personality. And He spared no pains to portray to us the caliber of this One.

If we are to appreciate fully the kind of person God is, if we are to grasp His essential love and goodness, if we are to understand even a little of the wonder of His winsomeness, if we are to know the strength of His integrity and reliability, then we must see Him as Christ saw Him.

Obviously God the Father completely dominated Christ's thinking. He influenced all of the Son's conduct. He occupied the prior place in all His affections. He was ever in His mind and on His lips.

One of the half-truths which plagues Christians is the old saying, "What you are speaks so loud, I cannot hear what you say." It is true, one's actions should correspond with one's words. But we can really only comprehend what a person's inner thoughts and life are like by what he says. "For out of the abundance of the heart the mouth speaketh" (Mt 12:34).

So if we are to fully grasp Christ's innermost thoughts and concepts of God as Father, we must, of necessity, pay careful attention to what He said about Him, as well as observe how Christ conducted Himself before His Father.

Jesus stated emphatically, "He that hath seen me hath seen the Father" (Jn 14:9). And we are most grateful for this personal, open revelation of God to us mortal men. In addition to His impeccable life, lived out before us on the stage of human affairs, we have as well His precepts and parables given to us for illumination. They are an endeavor to have us fully appreciate what God our Father is like.

There is no doubt that when Christ addressed God as His Father, it was in the full and splendid relationship of perfect Sonship. There was complete understanding. There was absolute agreement. There was total unity and harmony. There was deep delight.

But for us there is not always this open and unclouded approach to our Father.

We are haunted by our own misgivings. We are sometimes uneasy because of our own misconduct. We come rather gingerly because of our guilt. We wonder if we really will be understood because we are not sure we even understand ourselves. And often we question secretly if we will even be accepted.

Because of all this, it is essential to a reassuring and satisfying relationship with God that we study what His character is like. Unless we do begin to grasp what kind of person God is, we shall never fully develop a simple, strong confidence in Him. Yet, this is what He wants from us more than anything else, our trust and affection as His children.

The most outstanding attribute of our Father God is His love. There is a quality of selflessness and altruism to His character which is almost foreign to our finite human concept of love. So much of our love is self-centered. Often we are loving only when such conduct serves our own ends or satisfies our own selfish impulses.

With God, however, there is a love of magnificent and unchanging proportions. His care and concern and affection for us are not dependent upon His moods or our good behavior or our response to His overtures. Rather, it flows out to us in a clear, pure, powerful stream that has as its source and strength His own great heart of love. It is constant and unconditional.

Evidence of this lies in the fact that He Himself was willing to pay the penalty for our misdeeds. For God was in Christ reconciling the wayward world to Himself, not charging men's transgressions to their account (2 Co 5:19). And this He did for us through the death of His own dear Son while we were still alienated from Him.

Such a magnanimous gesture is almost beyond the bounds of our finite human comprehension. Nonetheless, it is an attested fact, which in itself undergirds our confidence in Him. It enables us to come to Him quietly, confidently, and without fear as, "Our Father." We can do this, not because of any merit on our part but rather because of His own generous attitude of concern and affection for us. We come freely because He has invited us to come, with an openhanded, greathearted welcome. But we can come and receive that welcome only through true repentance toward God and faith in His Son, the Lord Jesus Christ, as our Saviour. Only in this way can the Father-son relationship be established.

All too often God is viewed as a stern, austere Judge standing over us in an attitude of disdain and deprecation. We seem to see Him holding in His hands a giant set of scales. In it our bad deeds are weighed against our good conduct. And often we are filled with dismay at how our sins outweigh our good.

But this is a caricature of God our Father. It is a most distorted view of the One who loves us deeply and is able to enter fully and completely into our human dilemma. This is so because having made us, He understands our limitations and is sympathetic to our earthly struggles. He remembers that we are born and shaped in iniquity, that our brief sojourn upon the planet is a fleeting interval in which we struggle to cope with the assaults of sin and Satan upon our souls.

No, God our Father is not some distant deity who stands apart and aloof from the trials of men. He is not one to sit sternly in condemnation of His children. Rather, because He did identify Himself completely with us through the birth, life, and death of His Son our Saviour, He is touched with the feelings of our infirmities (Heb 2:16-18). He looks upon us in compassion and deep concern. He is moved by the least inclination on our part to resist evil and do good. And at every opportunity, He extends His helping hand to us by His gracious Spirit, eager to lift us up above the downward pull of evil.

Moreover, when we approach God, our Father, we are drawing close to Him who completely understands us. This is a concept which should give us enormous comfort and consolation.

It is an unfortunate fact that the great majority of human difficulties arise because we do not understand each other. At our very best, we humans are unpredictable. We can never fully understand why we do or say the things we do. No wonder we have so much conflict and chaos in interpersonal relations.

Besides our inability to understand others, no man or

woman fully understands even himself or herself. We cannot possibly unravel all the peculiar characteristics we may have acquired through complex hereditary processes from our parents. What makes one child in a family docile and agreeable while a brother or sister may be a self-willed young rebel?

Nor, likewise, can any person possibly determine the impact made upon his character by his parents or siblings during his formative years. At this critical time of life, all sorts of forces, unknown to him, have shaped the pattern of his future conduct. The influences of home, school, friends, teachers, parents, and casual acquaintances throughout one's life, condition his behavior, reactions, and outlook. Who can possibly understand all this? Certainly we cannot. At best we do not understand ourselves, let alone others. This is why so often we are so hard on ourselves and so harsh in our judgment and censure of others.

But this is not the case with the infinite, all-knowing God our Father. For He does know our makeup. He does understand why we are as we are. He does, in His all embracing tenderness, appreciate our particular problems. And because He does, He has a much more magnanimous attitude toward us than most of us have to ourselves or to each other (Ps 103:13-14).

It is for this reason that we can come to Him as our Father with the assurance that we will be given an understanding hearing. Unlike dealing with human beings, we will not be given short shrift. We will not be held in contempt. We will not be cut off or cut down with a critical attitude or cruel condemnation. Christ Himself reassured us of this when He emphasized that He had not come into the world to condemn men but to deliver them from their dilemma.

When we fully appreciate that the thoughts and inner attitudes of God toward us are good and gentle and understanding, what a difference it can make in our approach to Him. We come now, knowing full well that we shall be met with compassion and kindness, understanding and affection.

This reassures our hearts. It sets our minds at ease. It frees our spirits and releases us into a deep dimension of delight in our dealings with our heavenly Father. How good to know, here is someone who really understands; who knows all about us and who, even though He knows the worst, still loves us.

This explains why we can come to Him in any situation and find a warm welcome. It explains why we can count on a sympathetic hearing. Nothing else is so sure to dispel our fears and allay our anxiety as to know that in dealing with our Father, we are indeed dealing with a consistent character.

In human relations, all of us know that many of our problems arise because of the unpredictable nature of people. If a parent wakes up in the morning with a sick headache or upset stomach, it is more than likely the rest of the family will feel the brunt of the malady. We tend to vent our suffering and stresses on those around us. When a man is in a good mood and cheerful frame of mind, he will probably treat his children with great forbearance and leniency. But if, on the other hand, things are going wrong and he is in a bad mood, it is probable he will be harsh and hard with his family.

But there is none of this about God our Father. He is not fickle. He is not changeable. He is not subject to unpredictable fluctuations of temperament. He is always the same (Heb 13:8). Because of this, our relationship with Him can be a most beautiful thing. There is nothing else to compare with it in the whole realm of human relationships.

Only those who do truly know Him as Father are aware of how wonderful it is to be acquainted with such a being. For the rest, there lurks in the background of their minds the suspicion that somehow all of this is just too good to be true. They feel unsure of Him and unsure of others.

In order to convey this reliable aspect of God His Father's character to us, Jesus told the moving story of a father and his two sons (Lk 15:11-32). It is perhaps the most poignant parable in the gospels. The father's attitude toward both boys never altered, never changed. The young rascal subjected his father to appalling anxiety and awful anguish of heart. His dear old dad died a thousand deaths for that lad while he was away living it up. His father was no fool. He knew what the boy was doing in the distant land. Even the older brother knew that much. Not only was the father's fortune being squandered, but also his good name was being dragged in the dust. And on top of this, the old man's heart was being crushed relentlessly with sorrow.

Yet, despite all that the profligate son did to dismay his father, the parent's attitude toward him never deviated. In spite of all the shame, suffering, scandal, and loss, the father's love never diminished. Instead there went out from him forgiveness, compassion, love, and concern. At no time did he reject or repudiate his child. Despite all the boy had done, he was forgiven. He was never disowned or disinherited. And the day that broken, battered boy stumbled up the road toward home, he was met with the father's open arms and open heart that had never been shut against him.

The picture is replete with pathos and power. The

essence of the character of God our Father comes through to us here with no textual difficulty. The language is too clear, too simple, too potent for us to explain it away. This boy, despite all his misdeeds, had always been forgiven. All he had to do was come to his father and accept the forgiveness which was always there. The day he did this, he knew and felt fully accepted by his father. His misconduct was forgiven. The price and penalty for all his perverseness had been paid for in the suffering of his father.

This is what sets the forgiveness of God our Father on a plane far above that of us human beings. Not only has He forgiven us our misdemeanors, not only does He forget them, but He Himself bears the penalty of suffering which attends our misconduct.

The best of human beings, even when they find it within themselves to forgive another, seldom if ever can forget the wrong done to them. And, what is more, they expect that the one who committed the offense shall somehow, in due course, be made to pay the penalty for his misbehavior.

Even if we look at the relationship between the older of the two sons and his father, we find Christ conveying the same principle to our hearts. The elder brother, in his attitude of self-righteousness and self-pity had built a wall between himself and his father. All of his father's attempts to reach across that barrier had apparently been of no avail. He reassured the boy that everything he owned was his. In fact, according to tradition, he was entitled to twice as much as his younger brother because he was the firstborn son. His father's love and affection and interest in him were ever the same. But the poor fellow's pride and self-esteem prevented him from enjoying all the benefits at his disposal. This was simply because he did not believe what his father said. He was trying so hard to earn and merit by diligent service what was already rightfully his as the elder son.

His plight is almost the more pathetic of the two. It shows us a man who really never got to know his father. The picture painted for us is that of a person who sees God his Father, as someone harsh and hard and very demanding. He has never sensed His love, compassion, generosity, and fantastic forgiveness. And because he keeps his father at arm's length there has never been that wondrous sensation of feeling those open arms flung about him. He has never felt accepted. He has never felt wanted.

But just because the older boy took this attitude toward his father, it did not change the father's love and concern. For, after all, this lad too was still his son, his heir. He still yearned for him. He still reached out to him in tenderness. He still reassured him that everything he had was at his disposal if he would just come and accept it.

In the light of this account, we can see God our Father in a new and wondrous way, if we so choose. We can come to Him without reservations, no matter what our background may be. We can count on being accepted with warmth and wondrous delight.

Wrapped up in this little expression, "Our Father," lies a whole dimension of intimate companionship between father and child, between God and me. It reduces all the complications of life to a very simple, though very special relationship.

I sense that I am a child of God. I know assuredly that God is my Father and I am the object of His constant love and attention. There steals over my soul the realization that His concern and care for me are never ending, that

His patience and compassion and mercy and understanding are always extended to me. In every situation of life, no matter how unusual or adverse, there comes the quiet assurance to my heart that I am His and He is mine.

What a consolation! What an encouragement! What a stabilizing influence in my affairs!

It is little wonder that among the most favored phrases to fall from our Lord's lips, those of "Our Father," "My Father," "Father in heaven" held prior place. This concept and this relationship was the most precious He held in His heart. It provided the central meaning and direction to all of His life and ministry.

Throughout His earthly sojourn it is moving to note how often Christ referred to His Father. He saw Himself as here on earth completing His Father's will, carrying on His Father's work, complying with His Father's wishes, conversing quietly with His Father, while all the time making His way gently toward His Father's home.

This was the ever enduring hope and joy held before Him. It was the central relationship about which all the rest of His life and work revolved. And when the day dawns that we too see and know God truly as our Father, our walk and life with Him will have become one of great serenity and enormous import.

It is on this basis and against this sort of background that we can address God as our Father with confidence. We can come with the quiet assurance that He will be receptive of our petitions and appreciative of our gratitude.

There is no more beautiful nor meaningful manner in which to present our prayers, be they pleas for help or expressions of praise. Simply because He is our Father, we can expect that we shall be heard and our heart's communion will be reciprocated.

If Christ chose to preface His prayers in this intimate manner, then we may be quite sure we can do no better. It is fitting and appropriate that we come to God in an attitude that combines both respect and gentle endearment. No doubt this delights His heart. It is one of the honors we can bestow upon Him in return for the great honor He confers upon us by calling us His children (1 Jn 3:1-3).

There are times when we tend to take for granted the enormous privileges extended to us by being brought into the family of God. This is no small honor. There devolves upon us the responsibility to bear this family name with dignity and high esteem. This theme is developed in the prayer. Emphasis is placed upon the paramount prestige of God, as our Father, and the desire for us to comply with His desires and wishes in our conduct.

Our Father—just two short words. Yet they have a whole world of meaning wrapped up in them. They set the tone of this entire prayer. They embrace all the beauty to be found in a unified family. They convey to our hearts and minds the strength and serenity of the Almighty. They speak to our souls and spirits of the love that comes from an understanding Father's heart.

No other religion in all the world carries such a happy, contented concept of communion between God and man. No other philosophy or teaching so intimately touches the heart of our human needs. Where else can one turn to find words more tender, more meaningful, more mighty in their simplicity than *Our Father*.

Do we really know Him this way? We can!

TWO

Which Art in Heaven

"Who is in heaven."

The title of this chapter has been repeated deliberately in modern terminology. It has always seemed an enigma to me that the impersonal pronoun *which* should ever have been used for someone as personal and precious as "Our Father."

Unusual terminology is but one of many difficulties that have dogged the footsteps of those who, across the years, have endeavored to know God. Men and women of great sincerity and simple faith have had to struggle with the complexities and limitations of human language in their endeavor to understand divine truth. The marvel is that our grasp of our Father's mind and intentions toward us has been as broad and clear as it is despite the difficulties of human speech in its expression of abstract ideas.

If, for instance, the average person on the street, who had never been exposed to scriptural teaching, were to read the phrase, "Our Father which art in heaven," it would mean almost nothing to him. And even among those of us who have been accustomed to reading the Word of God in the more archaic form of English, there are those who are bewildered a bit by a simple statement

25

of this sort. The stark fact is that it is a phrase repeated glibly by millions of men and women who have never stopped to ask, what does it really mean? If pressed on the point they would scarcely know what to say.

Where is heaven? What is heaven? Is it a place? Is it a condition of life? Is it a different dimension of living? Is it far away or close at hand? These are all legitimate questions which deserve open and honest answers.

Too many of us are far too vague in our ideas about spiritual realities. If God is in heaven, then we ought to know something about heaven. If He is our Father and heaven is His natural environment, we should understand what that realm is really like.

The word *heaven* is derived from the old Anglo-Saxon word *heave-on*, meaning to be lifted up or uplifted.

So it implies the thought of a place or a state which is above that of the commonplace condition on earth.

Actually in the Scriptures, *heaven* is used to describe three rather distinct and different realms. First, we find it used over and over with reference to the earth's atmosphere. It is used to describe the envelope of air that surrounds the planet, conditions our climate, and sustains life. The formation of clouds, the precipitation of rain or hail or snow, the water vapor that provides mist and dew and frost, all are regarded as coming from heaven.

In other words, all that we normally associate with the atmosphere which enables life to flourish on the planet is said to be heaven. "For as the rain cometh down, and the snow from heaven, and returneth not thither, but watereth the earth, and maketh it bring forth and bud, that it may give seed to the sower, and bread to the eater" (Is 55:10).

Second, there is a very much broader sense in which the word *heaven* or *heavens* is used to describe outer space. It specifically refers to the sun, moon, stars, and sky. It denotes the unmeasured immensity of numberless galaxies flung across infinite expanses. It is used for the unending realm of stellar constellations that circle through the night in majestic movements. "The heavens declare the glory of God, and the firmament sheweth his handiwork. Day unto day uttereth speech, and night unto night sheweth knowledge. His going forth is from the end of the heaven, and his circuit unto the ends of it" (Ps 19:1-2, 6).

Finally there is a third heaven referred to throughout the New Testament as the realm of God. It is sometimes described as a definite place, a heavenly country, a New Jerusalem, a home prepared especially for God's children.

Paul wrote of a man who had been lifted up, or uplifted, into this third heaven and who declined to speak of it or even describe it. On the other hand, John, the grand old apostle and much loved prophet of God, went to great pains to recount all he had been shown of heaven in his Revelation.

Because of all this, it is not entirely surprising that there has been real bewilderment in the minds of many people about heaven.

We need to ask ourselves some very ordinary questions, to which we can give very honest answers. The Word of God says our Father is in heaven. Does this then mean He can be in the earth's atmosphere? Yes. Does it imply that He can occupy outer space? Yes. Does He inhabit the realm of the righteous? Yes. For God is a Spirit, able to be present anywhere and everywhere.

Is not the love of my Father, His concern and compassion for me, expressed in the gentle rain that falls upon the fields and forests, the meadows and the mountains? The air I breathe, charged with oxygen to energize my body, the water I drink to maintain my body metabolism, the food I eat to sustain my strength —where do they all originate? Are they not gifts from God, my Father? "Every good gift and every perfect gift is from above, and cometh down from the Father of lights, with whom is no variableness, neither shadow of turning" (Ja 1:17).

The sunrises and sunsets that flood the world in glory are deeply moving hours, hushed with the presence of our Father. The splendor of snow scenes, the incredible beauty of individual snowflakes or frost formations speak softly but surely of the One who has designed all of this with magnificent precision. The coming and going of cloud patterns with ethereal beauty and endless variety are but a reminder that *He is here.*

If we cannot see and sense and know the presence of our Father in the simple splendor of the earth's atmosphere around us, then how can we hope to know Him in some more mystical or superspiritual way?

He is everywhere present! He makes Himself apparent to us in a dozen different dimensions of daily contacts. The trouble is that most of us are too busy, too preoccupied with our own pursuits, too distracted by the gross materialism of our man-made world to pause and feel His hand upon us in the everyday environment of our lives.

When was the last time you went out alone to walk in the rain, your face uplifted, to let its freshness fall upon your cheeks? And, as you walked, did it dawn on your dull heart that this was a gentle reminder that all good gifts come from your Father? Or when was the last time that in breathless wonder you paused to humbly thank your Father for sharing some of His splendor with you in a glorious sunrise or glowing sunset?

It has been well said that the true measure of any man's spirituality is the degree to which he can detect God in the most simple events around him. It is no mere spiritual phraseology when Scripture declares, "They should seek the Lord, if haply they might feel after him, and find him, though he is not far from every one of us; For in him we live, and move, and have our being" (Ac 17:27-28).

There is such a thing as moving quietly and humbly through life, keenly aware and conscious of the fact that we are walking with God our Father. We sense that we are surrounded with His presence in the very air we breathe, the water we drink, the food we eat. We sense our souls being inspired and uplifted by the beauty and wonder of the environment which surrounds us. We sense our spirits quickened by that very intimate communion with our Father as He lifts us up and impresses our hearts with the beauty of sunshine and cloud, of the interplay of light and shadow on leaves, rocks, bark, sea, and sky. This is to know something of our Father in heaven, the heaven of the very natural but wondrous world around us.

What is true in sensing the presence of our Father in the immediate environment around us, applies equally to the vast reaches of outer space. The moon, planets, sun, stars, galaxies, and remote immensity of space are, despite their enormous distance from us, still very much a vital and moving part of our lives.

Who of us has not responded happily and eagerly to the warmth and brightness of sunlight. How it stirs us in spring after the long, drab, cold days of winter. Even animals and plants, trees and birds respond to its touch and turn themselves toward its life-giving rays. All the world seems a brighter and better place to live when it is bathed in the beauty of sunlight. This is one of our Father's kind gifts to all His earthborn creatures. Without it, life on the planet would end abruptly. This golden, light-energy transmitted across millions of miles of subzero space enables photosynthesis to proceed on the earth. And this is the basis of all life.

We accept such a phenomenon as a matter of course, but in fact it is of such complexity that even the most erudite scientists cannot fully comprehend it. For those of us who are the children of God, we look up, lift up our hearts and give thanks for so great a gift. It is to us another demonstration of our Father's care and provision for us as His people.

Our Saviour made some very startling remarks on this subject when He said, "Love your enemies, bless them that curse you, do good to them that hate you, and pray for them which despitefully use you, and persecute you; That ye may be the children of your Father, which is in heaven; for he maketh his sun to rise on the evil and on the good, and sendeth rain on the just and on the unjust" (Mt 5:44-45).

What has been said of the sun holds equally true of clear blue skies, whose splendor and brightness are a tremendous uplift to the human spirit. How our hopes soar and our hearts sing under clear skies. Again a gift from above.

In contemplating the glory and wonder of the night sky, most of us would admit freely that we have been moved by the magic of moonlight. The gentle touch of silver light that can soften the landscape and turn lakes, rivers, or ocean to quicksilver is one of the most serene sensations. Under the stars, in quiet night hours, the human heart can be very open to and very aware of the presence of our Father who is in heaven.

Our Father is very much in the heaven of outer space. He draws near to us in His own inimitable way and there speaks peace and comfort to our questing souls. The enormity and immensity of space may, it is true, tend to dwarf our spirits and humble our hearts before Him. But at the same time, we are reassured that He who could conceive and create such a unified and splendid universe deserves all of our devotion and adoration as His children. How good to know our Father is in His heaven and that He does in fact hold the whole world in His hands (Job 41:11).

Up to this point we have been dealing with two realms of heaven which are familiar to all of us, the earth's atmosphere and outer space. Now in order to understand something of that third realm, referred to in Scripture, as the third heaven (see 2 Co 12:1-7), we must turn our attention to a spiritual dimension of life.

Strange to say, we are not told as much about this heaven as we might wish. No doubt there is a very good and simple reason. I suggest sincerely it is because of our lifelong conditioning to an earthly existence, wherein our capacity to grasp or understand heavenly things is exceedingly limited.

It is akin to someone like myself, who loves the high, alpine country above the timberline in the Rockies, attempting to describe its delights to a group of little children from the slums of a great city. Never having been exposed to anything as beautiful as an alpine lake of exquisite blue or the fragile perfection of a mountain meadow carpeted in wild flowers, how could they imagine what I was describing? After the first few minutes, they would be lost and bewildered. So, to a degree, it is with us in considering the heaven of spiritual realities. We are so engulfed and surrounded by the sordid conditions of our own existence on earth, we can scarcely imagine being set free into a fresh, dynamic dimension of living, totally divorced from all that we know here.

Still our spirits do at times seek to comprehend a little of that realm. And so we set out to search the Scriptures and find out for ourselves what we can discover. What little I have been able to gather across the years is here shared with the reader. In doing so, no attempt is being made to be dogmatic. I am aware others may have quite divergent views to which they are fully entitled.

It was roughly seven years ago that my first, beloved wife, my companion of more than twenty years, was admitted to a cancer clinic. After her initial operation, the specialists called me in privately. They informed me she was stricken with the most virulent form of cancer known to science. In a few months her beautiful body and perhaps also her fine mind would be completely destroyed. There was no known way to counteract the awful ravages of the dread disease. The best I could do was to take her home and endeavor to make her final days as comfortable and easy as possible.

In such circumstances and at such an hour a man and woman, if they know God, are in deadly earnest to discover what heaven is all about. So, with death camping on our doorstep, we set out to search the Scriptures to see for ourselves what this third heaven was really like. After all, she would soon step through death's door to be home with the Lord. With a sense of anticipation and adventure upon us, we studied the Word of our God, and what we found gave enormous consolation and encouragement to our hearts.

Perhaps our most important discovery was that this third heaven is more than just merely a place; it also provides an entirely new dimension of living. It is a state in which God's children are set free from the cloying constrictions and limitations of their earthly life.

It includes being released from the crippling conditions common to our struggles here, into the enormous emancipation of a region and realm governed by God. It is to enjoy incredible freedom. In a word it means to be *free*.

The most astonishing aspect we found was that some fourteen (2 X 7) devastating difficulties which we contend with on earth are absent from heaven. Similarly there were seven delightful conditions present in heaven which are virtually unknown to men on earth. Quite briefly here are the twenty-one (3 X 7) aspects of heaven, deserving our careful consideration. As we examine them, it is well to remind ourselves that this is our Father's native environment. This is His natural abode. This is His home which He wants to share with us. And it is because He is in heaven that it is this way at all. It is His presence and His person which governs the conditions extant there.

1. We are set free from the assaults of our archenemy, Satan. In heaven the child of God no longer contends with the subtle insinuations and dark deceptions which the devil devises. His temptations and deceitful tactics are no more. What a glorious relief! Our doubting days are done. Our temptations are past.

2. The second aspect of our freedom is release from the strain of separation. We live in a world where the parting of ways and leave-taking of loved ones always

wrenches the heart and strains our emotions. But in heaven, this no longer poses a problem. Instead we are in an atmosphere of quiet contentment. We are finally at home. Our restless spirits are at rest because they have found their abode in God.

3. In heaven, we shall be free from tears of anguish, despair, and frustration. As C. S. Lewis points out in his book, *The Problem of Pain*, life carries with it more pain than pleasure. For many of God's children, the most bitter tears are those shed inwardly or alone where no one else sees the agony of our spirits. What a delightful deliverance to be free of such anguished moments!

4. In heaven there is no more death. Because of the power of our Father's eternal presence, and because of what Christ accomplished at Calvary, death cannot exist. For us who know God as our Father, death is but the doorway into His home. Still death hovers on the horizon of many lives. In our natural human condition we are still bound to ask, How will it come? Where? When? Most of us would prefer to pass on quietly into Christ's presence in our sleep. Most of us shrink from the dread thought of painful accidents or long and lingering disease prior to death. But in heaven, we will be free from this foreboding.

5. We shall enjoy total deliverance from the sorrow that is occasioned by regrets and remorse. At our best, we are bound to have made some grievous errors. We have entertained wrong attitudes, spoken unkind words, harbored selfish motives, and indulged in wrongful acts. Out of all this, there flows a muddied stream of remorse and sorrow. Yet, in heaven what a joy to know that we are fully forgiven, that we are free of folly and sorrow of spirit. Instead we shall be in a di-

mension of deep delight, free from the guilt and regret of our life's misdeeds.

6. John, the beloved apostle of Christ, also assures us that there is no crying in this wondrous realm—crying in the sense of a soul in search of truth, crying in the way that our hearts cry out for God. All of this will be gone. For in heaven the questing soul has at last come home to find our Father there waiting to welcome us, as always, with open arms.

7. The last of the first seven freedoms is our deliverance from pain. Surely it is wondrous enough to anticipate freedom from bodily, physical suffering. But how much more is the boundless pleasure of release from mental anguish and spiritual agony? Those conditions which plague our days and make of our nights a nightmare will have no place there. It scarcely seems possible, especially for those of us who, down through the long years of life's journey, have endured suffering of all sorts, including the agony of watching others, whom we love, grapple with the tyranny of pain.

All of this leaves us a bit breathless and amazed. Humanly, we cannot possibly imagine such a state of blessed relief. But we are given our Father's quiet assurance that this is what heaven is like. We scarce can take it in. Yet at this point we are still only one-third way through its wonders.

8. When God's new heaven, new earth, and New Jerusalem are unveiled, we will discover that in our new, eternal abode, there is no temple, no church, no sanctuary, no formal edifice or structure of any sort. *Structure* no doubt implies much more than a mere building. There will be a delightful, relaxed freedom between all God's people. Gone are the formal barriers and doctrinal divisions which divide us down here.

Among our Father's children will flow the warmth and love and understanding which only His divine presence can produce.

9. We are told too that there will be no sun or moon there. That is to say, no moon which we now know as the earth's satellite in the night sky. Nor will the sun, of which the planet earth is a satellite, be the dominant light of life. For in that realm, set free from our ties to this terrestrial sphere, time will be no more. No longer will we be limited by the time-space concept which conditions life on the planet earth.

This is almost beyond our imagination. From birth we are accustomed to think in terms of day and night, summer and winter, spring and fall. We grow up tied to time. We are always meeting deadlines and keeping appointments according to time. We set schedules, plan programs, and organize all of our lives around the clock and calendar. As the years go by, we sense our time, as sand in an hourglass, is running out. We feel a certain sense of helplessness as the years march on, inexorably taking their toll of our strength and stamina.

Over there, all of this will alter. Gone will be the sense of desperate urgency, of being crowded by the calendar, of being threatened by the tyranny of time. In its place will be the serene peace of a quiet and unhurried life, free from the fret and strain of earth's on-rushing pace. What a wondrous release!

10. Nor is there any night there. No doubt, in part, this implies physical darkness as we know it here. With new spiritual bodies, the need for night and sleep and restoration, so essential for our limited physical bodies, will no longer be a factor.

11. But over and beyond this, the night or darkness of misunderstanding will be banished. Perhaps of all the

magnificent deliverances promised to God's children, this is one of the most glorious. To think that at long last the misunderstandings, the darkness and clouds which so readily come between human beings, will be dispersed forever, is utterly beyond our grasp.

About eighty percent of the problems and perplexities that plague the human race are caused by misunderstandings which cloud our relationships. Most of us do not understand each other. We do not understand our Father in His dealings with us. We do not understand our own complex selves. Yet all of this will change. We shall enter an era of total and complete enlightenment. We shall know as we are known. There will vanish forever all the fears, doubts, misjudgments, animosities, and despair spawned in our present darkness of misunderstanding.

12. John also tells us that there is no defilement in that realm; nothing to contaminate our thoughts nor mar our moral life. It scarcely seems possible does it?

In our earthly society, at almost every turn we take, we are confronted with those influences which would besmirch our lives. We hear things which distort our minds and weaken our wills. We read about, see, handle those things which draw us away from our devotion to God. But in heaven these influences are no longer at play. They will cease to exert their influence on our lives.

Almost the same may be said for the perversion and corruption of the whole world system to which we are conditioned. We become so enmeshed in the affairs of life; we are so preoccupied with the never-ending struggle to earn a living, to provide for our families, that we forget how completely the world and its ways have dominated our thinking. But in our new home there is total deliverance from all the strain and stresses of our unpredictable earthly sojourn.

In his first epistle, John tells us, "Love not the world, neither the things that are in the world" (1 Jn 2:15). In heaven the attractions of the world system will no longer be present to defile us and drag us down. Their impact will be nil. What a deliverance!

13. Then, too, we are given to see that there will no longer be any deceit, falsehood, lies, or dishonesty there. To a large degree, all of us on earth have become accustomed to the deception, duplicity, and scheming which make up a part of our false fronts. We tend to live behind masks. We would have others believe that we are making a success of things. It is all one with the idea that we must not be seen in our true colors. We must not appear as failures. To do so is to lose face. And so even the best of us tend to say one thing yet mean another.

All of this will be at an end.

We shall be in the presence of the One who sees right through us. We can let down the front, take off the mask, and just be ourselves, both before God and before one another. What a relief! What a relaxation! The tension and suspense of all duplicity, contriving, and playacting will be past. What a rest for God's dear people.

14. Finally the fourteenth influence which will not be at work in our eternal home is sin. If all that has gone before us is a bit overwhelming, how much more this! Just think, the old, wearisome, never-ending downward pull of evil will have finally come to an end. It is a bit like suddenly finding ourselves set free from the pull of gravity.

It will be as though great lead weights have been unstrapped from our feet. We can walk freely, yes, even run, in the paths of righteousness. Imagine being no longer burdened down with the contamination of sin that clogs our feet, no longer loaded with the evil that stains our souls and starts our tears. Instead we will exult with lighthearted abandon. We will revel in the ecstasy of a new glory given us by our lovely Lord!

We have now examined the fourteen undesirable aspects of earth life not found in the home Christ has prepared for us. In the same way, there are seven beneficial aspects of that home which are not fully known to us in our earthly condition. This makes a total of three times seven, representing the ultimate in divine perfection.

Let us briefly examine these seven glorious concepts. Because they are so totally foreign to us, we can scarcely take them into our finite and very limited human understanding, but let us at least try.

1. There is a dimension of satisfaction and tranquillity not known here. It is epitomized by the pure water of life, clear as crystal that flows from the throne of God. A quality of life exists there, seldom if ever experienced by us here. It has to do with complete and enduring contentment and repose.

In our earthbound life, our best efforts, our finest endeavors, our loftiest achievements, still leave us a bit disappointed and disenchanted. No situation or circumstance, no matter how sublime, lasts long or remains free from some outside, corroding influence which tends to mar its brief bliss. The net result is that a sense of uncertainty hovers in the background of our best moments. We tell ourselves, "This is just too good to last." Not so in heaven. There, the very nature and unchanging character of our Father insures that our satisfaction shall be complete and continuous.

2. The second amazing attribute of heaven is its

abounding life. Life there has such an abundant quality that we really have nothing on earth with which to compare it. It is true that in our very best moments we may have a slight foretaste of it. But to imagine that such will be the norm there is enough to overwhelm us. To think that such things as absolute love, honesty, good-will, and righteousness make up the warp and woof of life in heaven is incredible. The more so after long years of coping with bitterness, hate, lies, deceit, and ill will in our human relationships.

There the ever present healing influence of God's own presence will be the balm that mends our broken spirits and heals our injured hearts.

3. The third thrilling aspect of heaven will be absolute justice and fairness which will characterize it. This obviously is so because God's throne is there. And where He rules, justice and righteousness reign.

Complete justice and fair treatment are seldom experienced in this world. On every side, we are dismayed by the injustices perpetrated between men and nations. Human beings are quick to exploit each other. We do not hesitate to take undue advantage of others whenever the opportunity arises. We are skilled and cunning in the way we use or abuse others for our own ends. But, in heaven, all that will end. Where God our Father reigns, so does righteousness and justice.

Gone will be discrimination, unfairness, scheming, conniving, and the smooth tactics and fast talk which take innocent people unawares. What a relief!

4. Surprising as it may seem, the fourth feature of heaven will be our service to God Himself. Put in ordinary layman's language, all the work we do there will have special significance and deep meaning, for it will be divine.

Just what form it will take we are not told exactly. It really does not matter that much, for, whatever its nature, it will be good. From experience, we know that much of our work here is pretty pointless. In fact, millions of men and women live lives "of quiet desperation." Life is one, long, tedious bore. All their efforts, energy, time, intelligence, and attention are directed to work which they find empty and meaningless.

In eternity, our service will be different. Life there takes a new turn. It assumes a new direction. The smallest action will be linked to a divine destiny. And from that linking, there will emerge a series of delightful enterprises in which men and God are active co-workers.

5. The fifth aspect is exquisite fellowship. This is perhaps the best known and most commonly accepted attribute of heaven. We here live life by faith. There we shall see our heavenly Father face to face. The joy of such an encounter will be tremendous.

Because all of us shall be exposed to such an intimate contact there is no question but that it will bind us together in a common fraternity and family atmosphere. Our Father will preside over His adoring children, and we, in turn, will be doubly attracted and drawn together in the presence and power of His own gracious person. His character and love will draw us all close together, making us one with Himself.

6. By virtue of this very full and complete revelation and disclosure of Himself, it is natural that there will be a full and complete illumination of every aspect of life. No longer will or could there be doubts, misgivings, or apprehension of any sort.

Because we are beleaguered by so much doubt and misunderstanding here, it is almost impossible to project our thoughts or imagination to a realm where all will be bright and right. To live and move and have our being in such a dimension is beyond our most optimistic hopes. We will be set free from all the fears and forebodings which attend our days here. And this is simply because God our Father is in heaven.

7. The last and seventh positive aspect of heaven is, in a way, its most comforting to the child of God. It is the realm of victory. It is the place of rest at last. It is the dimension of life where the battles, struggles, and contest with sin and Satan and self are all over, and the warrior of the Lord has come into His inheritance. We are told we shall reign for ever and ever with Christ. It seems almost too good to be true, but like all the other promises of God our Father, we can count on it.

Looking back over this long list of heaven's attributes, it is important to remind ourselves again that this is our Father's native realm. It is His natural environment. It is His home and habitat. Heaven is what it is by virtue of the fact that His presence, power, conduct, and character make it such.

We have been taught very clearly in Scripture that Christ is pleased to come into any life where He is invited (see Jn 14:23 and Rev 3:20). He takes up residence there and makes real in that life His very nature and person.

This is a very crucial concept in the Christian life. It can make all the difference between a victorious Christian and a very indifferent Christian.

If Christ resides within my heart, by His Spirit, then there should be a foretaste, at least, of heaven in my life down here. Some of us have known blessed days in our experience, when, from dawn to dusk, we appeared to behave, think, and speak exactly as Christ would have us to do. At the end of the day, we could look back and know assuredly that to have so lived was in fact to have had a brief preview of heaven.

When, in teaching the disciples this magnificent prayer, Jesus said, "Our Father, who is in heaven," He was not thinking of a distant being in some remote heaven. He was referring to One whose existence was a vital part of His own life.

What was true of Christ as He lived in Palestine twenty centuries ago, can and may be equally true of us today.

"Our Father, who is in heaven," is also in my heart. To know this is to know a new dimension to life. To sense the presence and person of God our Father within is to have set our feet on the highway to heaven. But, even more than that, we will see our lives now as the residence and habitation of the Most High. We will know ourselves to be host to our heavenly Father. And in such knowing there will steal over us a quiet awe and deep respect for our Father who deigns to have His Son come and share Himself with us as Lord and King.

In Luke 17:20-21, Jesus was asked where was the Kingdom of God. His forthright reply was, "It is within you."

Once God's sovereignty has been established in any human heart, the establishment of an environment that resembles heaven itself follows within that life.

Unless we have experienced something of this sort and feel somewhat at home with God down here, it is less than likely that we would ever feel comfortable over there. Some people hold the preposterous notion that they can do pretty well as they please in this life, then still have hope of feeling at ease in heaven. Not likely!

Unless a man or woman has accepted Jesus as Saviour

and thus knows God as Father in this world, he would not feel at home in heaven. This is a most solemn and serious consideration. And, I am sure, it was one of the thoughts in our Master's mind when He taught His disciples to pray, "Our Father, who is in heaven [here and now]."

In layman's language, what He was implying was this: "Seek to know God as your Father here. Let heaven begin now in this life."

And this can be so if we wish it to happen.

THREE

Hallowed Be Thy Name

"Hallowed be thy name."

A very positive, potent statement. What does it mean? What is implied in this affirmation? It is not just a petition. Nor is it just a pious hope, as if to say in passing, "May Your name be honored."

The concepts in Christ's mind, when He inserted this declaration into His prayer, were tremendously important to Him. It was not a casual bit of religiosity for Him to insist that God's name be hallowed. Rather, there was inherent in this four-word phrase, a whole world of respect, reverence, awe, and appreciation for the person of God His Father.

The word *name*, as used here by Christ, is not restricted to being a title. It means much more than just a surname, or given name, such as *George Macdonald*, might be used as a means of identifying a single human being. In Scripture, the name of God implies a very much greater concept.

"Thy name"—God's name—implies the title, person, power, authority, character, and the very reputation of God.

So enormous was the respect of the ancient Hebrew people for the name of God that they dared not even formulate it with their lips nor attempt to put it into human language. It was represented in writing by the letters Y H W H. Later these were expanded to Y A H-W E H, which became the name *Jehovah*, and in our English translations, it is represented by the expression "the LORD" (e.g., KJV and NASB).

Obviously the eternal God, the One who is from ever-lasting to everlasting, could scarcely be identified by any simple human title.

Again and again when asked who He was, the simple reply that came back was, "I AM THAT I AM." Even Jesus, when pressed on this point replied, "Before Abra-ham was, I am" (Jn 8:58). By this it was intended to make clear that God is the eternal, enduring, everlasting Lord of all the universe, both heaven and earth. Because He, our Father, is from everlasting to everlasting the same, He deserves our utmost respect and reverence.

Yet, as pointed out in the first chapter, the amazing disclosure of His person, given to us by Christ, was not that of some distant, remote, unapproachable deity. Rather the revelation of Jesus regarding God that dispels our fears and warms our hearts is that He is in fact our Father, all compassionate, understanding, and totally approachable.

It is in the light of this revelation that the name of God our Father takes on a whole new dimension of devotion for us. We are not so much concerned here with the mere formality of His title, as we are with the quality of His person, character, and reputation.

Putting it into plain language, what Jesus is saying in this prayer is, "Father, may Your person, Your identity, Your character, Your reputation, Your very being al-ways be honored."

The significance of such a statement may not have

any special meaning for us unless we understand something of the caliber of God's character. I say this because, unless we do, the idea of keeping His name hallowed will have little or no importance.

God our Father is the most balanced being. He cannot in any way be compared to nor equated with human beings, who, at best are far from being balanced. In fact we are so twisted and distorted in our characters that we have difficulty trying to comprehend the beautiful character of our Father.

Actually it is our heavenly Father's character which is His great glory. Or, conversely, we may say that His glory is His character.

To help grasp this, I sometimes think of His character in the form of a perfectly symmetrical six-sided cube. On one side, He is utterly holy, pure, and flawless. But this is counterbalanced on the opposite side by His absolute love, compassion, and concern. Only because of this is it possible for us to approach such a sublime being. On a third side, He is completely righteous, just, impeccable. Yet again this is counterbalanced on the fourth side by His boundless mercy, kindness, and long-suffering. If it were not so, how could we ever stand in His presence? He is also, on the fifth side, utterly, honest, true, and reliable, again, counterbalanced on the sixth side by His infinite faithfulness, understanding, and interest in us as His children.

Such a character and such a person, if we even catch the faintest glimpse of His goodness, is bound to elicit our fondest affection and deepest gratitude. No wonder we are bound to exclaim, "We love him, because he first loved us!" (1 Jn 4:19). And it was this thought in Christ's mind which prompted Him to say, "Hallowed be thy name," or, "May Your very being be revered."

It will be recalled that this concept was the very heart and impulse of the early Church. Everything that small band of believers set out to do was always "In the name of Christ" or "In the name of Jesus of Nazareth." For in that name, there was vested all the power, dynamic, authority, prestige, and import of the character of the living Lord.

To help us get a grip on this idea, let us compare it to our modern concept of what can be implied by a name in business. Take, for example, the name *Rolls Royce.* When we see that name stamped on an automobile or an aircraft engine, we immediately have a special regard and respect for it. In that name resides the reputation of one of the world's most renowned engineering firms. That name stands for the finest in mechanical engineering. It represents the most advanced research. It bears the stamp of meticulous care and precision. It symbolizes the ultimate in reliability and dependability. It denotes the highest degree of craftsmanship and design.

Now if this be true in the case of a human enterprise that has earned an enviable reputation, how much more so must the same principle apply to our Father in heaven, Creator of the whole, wondrous universe.

All of this was in our Saviour's mind and heart as He formulated this simple yet profound prayer.

The word *hallowed* has been used in most of our English translations to convey the idea Christ was teaching here. Unfortunately *hallow* is not in common use today. It is associated with the word *holy,* which again seems to be grossly misunderstood by most modern readers. For us to say, "Father in heaven, may Your name be kept holy," sounds very trite. It smacks of musty, dim churches. It conjures up before our minds sad, mournful, almost morbid music. We associate it with cloistered halls, long robes, dismal chants, halos, and all the other tired traditions that somehow have been unfortunately identified with this idea of God being holy.

The word *holy* is derived from the old Anglo-Saxon words *halig* or *hale*. And these were used to denote that which was either set apart, very special, sound, healthy, or whole.

For instance, it is not uncommon to hear people say, "Oh, I'm hale and hearty," meaning that the person is in excellent health, wholesome, and fit.

So that basically when something is said to be holy, the first idea is that of being completely sound, solid, whole, healthy and wholesome, without blemish, weakness, soft spots, and without in any way being defiled or contaminated.

Following on this naturally comes the thought that anything or anyone holy was unique and unusual, set apart, free from defilement of any sort. So it may be seen that to speak of keeping God's name holy really embraces a very broad and sweeping appreciation of who He is and what He does.

What we would say in modern idiom is something like this: "May You be honored, revered, and respected because of who You are. May Your reputation, name, person, and character be kept untarnished, uncontaminated, unsullied. May nothing be done to debase or defame Your record."

In Isaiah 6, we are given a very dramatic and moving description of the prophet's impressions of the holy God. "I saw also the Lord sitting upon a throne, high and lifted up, and his train filled the temple. Above it stood the seraphim: each one had six wings; with twain he covered his face, and with twain he covered his feet, and with twain he did fly. And one cried unto another, and said, Holy, holy, holy, is the Lord of hosts; the whole earth is full of his glory. And the posts of the door moved at the voice of him that cried, and the house was filled with smoke. Then said I, Woe is me! For I am undone, because I am a man of unclean lips, and I dwell in the midst of a people of unclean lips; for mine eyes have seen the King, the Lord of hosts" (Is 6:1-5).

In the presence of the Almighty God, Isaiah became keenly aware of his own blemishes. The person and power and purity of the Holy One made him acutely conscious of his own contamination. It is in the intense and glowing wholesomeness of God's person that our own weakness and defilements appear their worst. The nearer we draw to Him, the more acutely we sense our own sinfulness. And this is as it should be, for only then do we discover our real need of cleansing from our own uncleanness.

Our society today is no different, basically, than that of Isaiah's day, nor of our Lord's day, when He taught His disciples this prayer. No matter what generation we are a part of, men and women in general do not revere nor respect the name and person of the Most High. That is partially why it was important for Jesus to put this phrase into the prayer.

Irrespective of what strata of society we move among, it is very common for men and women to degrade and defile God's name. His name is used in blasphemy. It is used in obscene jests; His character is lampooned and ridiculed; His person is heaped with insults and abuse equal to anything hurled at Christ during His mock trial and cruel crucifixion. From very small children to white-headed old men and women there races a continuing stream of scorn, sarcasm, sneering, and cursing against the Holy One.

Why this should be has always baffled me. The only adequate explanation I can find is that it is the very beauty, loveliness, wholesomeness, and purity of His wondrous character that makes human beings uncomfortable. His sublime attributes and person and name, instead of eliciting reverence and awe, draw out hostility, anger, and malice from men.

It is little marvel that among the first ten written commandments given by God to men there should have been included, "Thou shalt not take the name of the LORD thy God in vain" (Ex 20:7).

So in a sense, Jesus Christ, was reaffirming this thought when in His prayer He said, "Hallowed be thy name." This, of course especially applies to those of us who, not out of a sense of duty to the Law, but out of love and esteem for our Father in heaven, wish it that way. Not only do we wish it, but, much more, we see to it that His wondrous name is honored.

As in the case of Isaiah, so in ours. There are those great areas of life wherein it is essential that God's reputation and person be recognized and respected. These are, first, the world at large, for Isaiah records that the Seraphim's cry was, "Holy, holy, holy, is the LORD of hosts; *the whole earth is full of his glory.*" Or in other words, everywhere, all around us, there is made apparent the presence and power and character of God our Father.

Second, there is the whole area of the Church, the sanctuaries set apart for the Most High, the body of believers wherever they be and wherever they meet. Again Isaiah records "I saw also the Lord sitting upon a throne, high and lifted up, and his train filled the temple." His person and authority and honor were everywhere apparent in the sanctuary.

Third, there is the immediate area of our own lives and our innermost relationship to the Most High. Isaiah sensed that because of his own uncleanness, he was unworthy of the holy God with whom he communed. But after he had been cleansed, purified, and his iniquity removed, he knew he could have intimate fellowship with God. And it was with this awareness of having been accepted that he went out to deliver God's message to hard hearts.

When we consider the world at large, we face the fact that in general our Father's name is certainly not hallowed. In fact for many, even among those who do not openly blaspheme Him, He appears to be either dead or at best of little consequence at all. Especially is this true of our Western civilization. Here science and twentieth-century technology have usurped the throne of men's minds. Most of our people have been conditioned to believe that God really does not matter. Of so little importance is He that no time is even given in classrooms to consider His role in human history.

The common concept abroad today is that it is man, with his inquiring mind and huge research programs, who is discovering and inventing the intricate complexities of natural science. Technology is well nigh worshiped. Yet the naked truth is that all man really does is to uncover laws, principles, and concepts which were brought into existence eons ago. And for every door the scientist unlocks, he finds a half dozen more waiting to be opened. So really there is no end to the acquisition of knowledge. A moment's serious and honest reflection will reveal that this vast store of incredible information was first programmed, established, then set in motion by a superior intelligence, the divine mind and sublime power of our heavenly Father.

This is why whenever I am afield or outdoors, there steals over me the acute consciousness that I am confronted on every hand by the superb workmanship of my Father. It is as if every tree, rock, river, flower, mountain, bird, or blade of grass had stamped upon it the indelible label, "Made by God." Is it any wonder that in a simple yet sublime sense of devotion, respect, and reverence for all of life, Christ longed for His Father's name to be hallowed throughout the earth. After all it is His realm.

At least for me, as His child, there remains the quiet joy and pleasure of walking and living very humbly with Him whose superb and beautiful craftsmanship surrounds me on every side. This lends enormous dignity to my days here.

As I pen these lines, it is a sun-dappled day in the lovely lake country of British Columbia. The high hills across the lake lie in their own deep blue shadows. Cloud patterns drift across the wind-stirred waters. The call of wild Canadian geese is borne above the shore cliffs on the breeze. And all around, green grass springs from soil warmed by April's sunshine. Man and all his inventions have had no part in producing a single one of these glorious sensations. All of them have come directly from the creative hand of my Father in heaven. Little marvel I often bow my heart in quiet adoration and gratitude to whisper, "How great Thou art!"

When we come to consider the aspect of reverence and respect which should be given to God in the church, it would seem this should be natural. The reader may well ask, "Isn't that what the church is for, a place to worship God? Why bother even discussing it?"

The truth is that there are too many churches where His name is not hallowed. This is not written in an attitude of censure. It is merely to state the case as it exists. The concept that the sanctuary is a sacred place where men and women come to have a personal and profound encounter with the living God is rapidly passing from our modern approach to worship.

Very often the program, special music, latest social function, architecture of the building, or even the preacher's personality are considered of far more importance than the authority and person and presence of God Himself. His name is not honored in these places. His being and power are not revered. And in some cases, the people are scarcely even aware of His character.

It is not altogether surprising, therefore, that many churches are little more than another social organization in the community. For where our heavenly Father's name is not held high, the church loses its impact and power upon the lives of its people.

The late A. W. Tozer, who wrote at great length about the life of the modern church, maintained that its greatest loss today was the loss of reverence for God Himself. It was his firm conviction that God would honor any group of believers who honored Him. Whereas, wherever He was neglected or relegated to some mere religiosity, death and decadence were bound to follow.

Like the ancient prophet Isaiah, we would do well to have our spiritual eyes opened to see God's very presence pervading His temple. We would do well to worship reverently. And we would do well to remind ourselves always that God our Father deserves our sincere and honest respect, our deepest gratitude.

Finally, let us consider one last but perhaps most

important aspect in which our Father's name needs to be hallowed and honored within our own personal lives. It follows, does it not, that if God is our Father, as Jesus expressed it in this prayer, then we are His children? And if we are His children, then naturally we ourselves bear His name. We may call ourselves "children of God," "Christians," "God's people," or any other such title. But the point remains that we carry His name. His name is vested in us. Therefore His name, reputation, person, and character are at stake in us.

It may very well be that a cynical and materialistic society will neither look for nor even expect to see God our Father in the natural world. Many of them are too cynical or totally indifferent to look for Him in the church. Yet, in a most surprising way, they will scrutinize anyone meticulously who claims to be a child of God.

The personal life and language of any person who says he is related to God comes in for close and continuous examination by an onlooking world. Not only do they expect much more of us, but, strangely enough, they almost demand perfection. This is one of those peculiar quirks in human nature so difficult to understand. Although almost anything goes for them, from God's children, they expect angelic conduct.

In large part, I am convinced this is simply because one dares to bear the name of our Father who is in heaven. So their attitude is, "If you claim to be a child of God, live like it!" No doubt Christ Himself was acutely aware of this attitude. That is why He urged His followers to live life on such a lofty and noble plane that men "may see your good works, and glorify [honor] your Father, which is in heaven" (Mt 5:16).

This is a very tall order indeed, for, human nature

being what it is, people will find fault with even the best of men. It is impossible to please everyone. Anyone who tries to do so ends up pleasing no one. Jesus Himself pointed this out one day. Because of His own open, warmhearted and genial attitude to the social customs of His day, He was dubbed "a glutton and winebibber, a friend of publicans and sinners." John the Baptist, on the other hand, whom Jesus declared "the greatest man ever born of a woman," was derided as "having a devil" by his detractors because of his own abstemious habits (Mt 11:17-19).

Still this does not excuse the people of God from living life in such a way that their Father's name shall be honored in their life and conduct. It is as if we were to pray each morning, "Father, Your reputation is at stake in me today. May I live in such a way as to do Your person great credit. Because of my behavior, may men see You in me, and so honor Your name because of it."

Throughout the Old Testament, and especially in the Psalms and Proverbs, great emphasis is placed upon reverence and respect for God our Father. It is pointed out repeatedly that to honor God and to accord Him prior place in our lives is the beginning of wisdom and the basis of all blessings from above. Over and over, the idea is impressed upon God's people that anyone who gave Him the esteem He so rightly deserved was bound to benefit to a degree beyond his wildest dreams.

Some of us forget this in our relationship to God our Father. Sometimes we may even be inclined to hold somewhat of a grudging attitude toward Him. We behave as though it is a bit of a burden and rather a bore to reverence and respect our heavenly Father. We are reluctant to honor Him.

Those of us who are human parents know how very

Those of us who are human fathers know how very hurt we can be by such an attitude from our own children. Yet, on the other hand, when they act toward us in gratitude and appreciation, when they express their love and respect for us in consideration and affection, how our hearts are warmed! It is then our own love for them is multiplied and aroused to the point that we are willing and eager to do even more for them than ever before.

The same principle applies in our relationship to our Father in heaven. The least movement on our part, feeble as it may seem, to honor and uplift His great name, produces an immediate response of love in His great heart. We find ourselves engulfed by His sublime presence through His Spirit. We discover our lives enriched by boundless blessings beyond our fondest hopes. This is just the way it is with our Father when His name is honored.

FOUR

Thy Kingdom Come

"Thy kingdom come."

Like the phrase "Our Father," or, "My Father," which was so often on the Master's lips, so the phrases, "the Kingdom of God," or, "the Kingdom of heaven" were frequently uppermost in His thoughts and teaching. It is no wonder then, that He would introduce this theme into His prayer. It was such an important concept that He makes it a very pointed petition to God, His Father: "Thy kingdom come!"

A great deal of doctrinal discussion has surrounded the term *Kingdom of God* or *Kingdom of heaven.* It is not intended here to compound the difficulties concerning the subject. Rather an honest and sincere endeavor is made to explain the theme in laymen's language. Hopefully this will make its meaning clear and more helpful in our relationships to God as our Father.

Even in the time of Jesus, His most ardent followers had real difficulty in comprehending the Kingdom of God. Most of them were quite sure it referred to an earthly empire which He would establish. The people of Israel were weary with the burdens and angry at the abuse they bore under Rome's rigid rule. They were convinced Christ was their great, new, emerging monarch who, by supernatural force, would overthrow the oppressor. They were positive the might of the foreigners would be shattered, and they would be set free again.

Because of this implicit belief, the disciples especially were utterly baffled and beaten by the final bewildering sequence of events that led their Lord to a criminal's crucifixion at Calvary. It seemed strangely impossible to them that their Messiah, their Christ, their Anointed One, should suddenly meet an ignominious end. After all, was not the "Kingdom of heaven" always on His mind and heart? Yet now it had suddenly come to nothing!

That they had misinterpreted His teachings was obvious, in spite of the fact that at one point Jesus went to the trouble to explain clearly that the Kingdom of God was more than an institution of physical composition, but was also a structure that could not be apprehended with one's ordinary finite faculties.

Being asked by the Pharisees when the Kingdom of God was coming, Jesus answered, "The kingdom of God does not come that you can watch closely for it. Nor shall they say, 'See here!' or 'See there!' for the kingdom of God is within you!" (Lk 17:20-21, Weymouth).

Even John the Baptist, despite his enormous spiritual insight, somehow failed to fully grasp what Christ meant by the Kingdom of God. From the depths of his despair in Herod's dungeon, he sent some of his disciples to discover whether Jesus was in fact the coming King whom he had heralded. Again and again, the rugged, fearless prophet had thundered in the wilderness, "Repent; for the kingdom of heaven is at hand" (Mt 3:2). And, what was more, the Messiah Himself had picked

up exactly the same refrain and began His public ministry by declaring, "Repent; for the kingdom of heaven is
at hand" (Mt 4:17).

Yet here, all of this emphasis on the coming kingdom
had apparently come to nothing. All the teaching, parables, discourses dealing with the Kingdom of heaven,
had, it seemed, only confused and confounded Christ's
followers.

And, in some measure, it is true to say that the Kingdom of God, even to this day baffles people. For example, there are those who assert that "the Kingdom of
heaven," referred to throughout Matthew's writing, is
quite distinct from "the Kingdom of God" spoken of by
Mark, Luke, and John.

Others contend that "the Kingdom of heaven" is some
future, divine dynasty that is to be established on earth.
They say it is of special significance only to the Jews,
who, still awaiting their promised Messiah, will eventually see His righteous government in control of the
world.

Other scholars assert that "the Kingdom of God" is the
social activity and outreach of the Church during this
era of human history.

When Jesus uttered the simple request to His Father,
"Thy kingdom come," He was not only thinking of the
Messianic kingdom, but also implied that He was invit-
ing Him to establish His Kingship in the hearts and lives
of men. In fact, when any human being utters this
prayer, if it is done in sincerity, it conveys the request to
have divine sovereignty, God's government, set up in a
human life.

But, perhaps another way to express this thought
clearly, is to say we are asking for God's Kingship to
become paramount, His sovereignty to become supreme

in our personal, private lives as well as in the ages to come.

The reader, unless he comes from a country where the king or queen are sovereign, may have some difficulty grasping this idea of a kingdom. But it should be understood that no king is a king without a kingdom to rule over. No sovereign is a sovereign without a state under his control. Even though the ruler may be deposed, dethroned or even exiled, he is still sovereign by right of rule over a state or territory or kingdom.

So what our Lord is saying in this prayer is, "Our Father . . . in heaven, hallowed be thy name; thy kingdom come," meaning, "You, oh God, our Father, who art Ruler of heaven and earth, whose authority is utterly paramount throughout the universe, come and establish Your sovereignty as well in the hearts of us men on earth, and eventually upon the earth itself."

Now this is a fairly simple statement that any human being can make rather glibly. It is made millions of times every year without any serious intention of having it happen. People pray it but do not mean it.

There is far too much at stake. The great majority are utterly unwilling to surrender the sovereignty of their lives to God. They have no intention whatever of abdicating the throne of their own inner wills and hearts to the King of Glory. They are no more prepared or willing to accept the rulership of Christ than were those who shouted at His crucifixion, "We have no king but Caesar!"

When all is said and done, most of us from our earliest childhood believe we are the king of our own castle. We determine our own destinies; we arrange our own affairs; we govern our own lives. We become supreme specialists in selfish, self-centered living where all of life revolves around the epicenter of *me, I, mine.*

So, if I sincerely, earnestly, and genuinely implore God to come into my life and experiences, there to establish His Kingdom, I can only expect that there is bound to be a most tremendous confrontation. It is inevitable that there will follow a formidable conflict between His divine sovereignty and my self-willed ego.

When I pray, "Thy kingdom come," I am willing to relinquish the rule of my own life, to give up governing my own affairs, to abstain from making my own decisions in order to allow God, by His indwelling Spirit, to decide for me what I shall do.

Paul emphasized this concept in 1 Corinthians 3:16: "Know ye not that ye are the temple of God, and that the Spirit of God dwelleth in you?"

Also, "Ye are the temple of the living God; as God hath said, I will dwell in them, and walk in them; and I will be their God, and they shall be my people. Wherefore, come out from among them, and be ye separate, saith the Lord, and touch not the unclean thing; and I will receive you, and will be a Father unto you, and ye shall be my sons and daughters, saith the Lord Almighty" (2 Co 6:16-18).

So when Christ uttered the simple yet profound petition, "Thy kingdom come," He envisaged His own future kingdom on earth and also the very Spirit of the living God coming into a human heart at regeneration to make it His holy habitation. He pictured the King of kings so permeating and invading a life that His authority would be established in that person's mind and will. He saw a human being as a temple, an abode, a residence of the Most High. But He knew that only when such an occupied heart is held and controlled by the indwelling

Spirit could it be truly said that here indeed is a part of the spiritual Kingdom of God where His will was done on earth.

Of course, such a relationship conveys with it enormous benefits and privileges. It is no small thing to be a member of this select, spiritual community. It is a most lofty and noble honor to be counted among the citizens of God's heavenly Kingdom. It is even more amazing to think there is bestowed upon us the special distinction of being God's people.

It is probably true to say that most of us who have invited Christ to come into our lives by His Spirit are not sufficiently aware of *who* it is that has established residence within us. This one is *royalty*. This one is the *King of kings*. This one is the *Lord of lords*. He is the *Prince of peace*. For the gracious Spirit of God, who indwells our beings, is none other than the representative of the risen and living Christ.

An acute awareness of this fact can revolutionize our whole life. A keen sense of God's presence within can change our entire outlook, alter all our attitudes, redirect all our activities.

The basic difference between a defeated, dismal Christian and a victorious, vibrant Christian lies in whether or not God, by His Spirit, controls the life. If He has there taken up sovereignty as well as residence in the soul, establishing a bit of the Kingdom of God in this human heart, that person will know the presence of God which will transform his entire being. It will become to him a delight to do God's bidding. It will be to him an honor to be God's subject.

Perhaps an experience from my own boyhood will help the reader to grasp the greatness of this theme.

I was born in Kenya, when it was considered one of

the remote, far-flung, frontier segments of the then mighty British Empire. In those days, it took weeks and weeks of tedious sea travel from Britain to reach this little-known country on the East Coast of Africa. The few white people in the colony were a rough-and-tumble band of frontiersmen with a rather casual allegiance to the distant British king in London.

Through force of circumstances, I was sent off to a distant boarding school, hundreds of miles from home. There, with a ragtag group of other frontier youngsters, I was given a rudimentary education. The school sat on a bleak, windswept hillside, looking out over the wild, wide African plains.

One day, the whole country was suddenly electrified with the startling news that the colony was to be visited by royalty from London. In fact King George V had, in response to our request, agreed to send his son, the Prince of Wales, to take up residence in Kenya. We were to receive royalty!

Never before had I seen such elaborate and painstaking preparations for anyone's arrival. We rough-and-ready youngsters were scrubbed and brushed until we shone. Our clothes were washed and ironed to perfection. Our rough boots were cleaned and polished until they glistened.

Finally the tremendous day for the prince to arrive had come. We were carefully instructed that, as his loyal subjects, we were to march down to the little dusty railway station where his royal train would stop. There we would stand at attention and present ourselves to him as his people. "The prince is coming! The prince is coming!" was the cry of excitement and elation on our lips.

Finally the royal train rolled into the little frontier

station. We boys and men stood stiffly at attention. All the girls and ladies, erect and beautiful in gorgeous white gowns, were alert with eager anticipation. The prince stepped from the train. Graciously he walked up and down our little lines, greeting us personally and proudly. He had come to his people, his subjects. He had come among us to take up residence. He was establishing a bit of the British Empire, a bit of his father's kingdom, right there in that untamed, foreign soil of Africa.

It was explained to us that the keys to the city of Nairobi, the capital of Kenya, were to be handed over to him. We had thus, as his subjects, turned over the control of our country to him. He was to set up a bit of Britain on African soil. Since he was the king's son and his personal representative, it was exactly the same as if the king himself was in residence among us. The king had come!

It was a grand event in the life of the whole country. It bound us to the British crown and to our king as no other action could have done. We had received royalty!

And the test of our loyalty was soon to be made, when war broke out and most of us were glad to give ourselves freely for king and country. We were then faithful subjects, glad and willing to obey our king's commands.

This, without doubt, is the concept and picture held so clearly in our Lord's heart when He prayed to His Father: "Thy kingdom come. Thy will be done."

Bishop Taylor Smith, that great and godly bishop in the Church of England, put into one of his personal memos a moving statement of his own relationship to the Kingdom of God. He said, "As soon as I awake each morning I rise from bed at once. I dress promptly. I wash myself, shave and comb my hair. Then fully attired, wide awake and properly groomed I go quietly to my study. There, before God Almighty, and Christ my King, I humbly present myself as a loyal subject to my Sovereign, ready and eager to be of service to Him for the day."

To live thus is to know something of the Kingdom of God on earth. Is it any wonder this man's life made such an impact for God? How many of us conduct ourselves this way before our King?

When there steals over our spirits an acute awareness that God does in fact choose to reside within us, it is not nearly so difficult to vacate the throne of our own lives in His favor. We find it is a joy to pay deference to Him. As with David, we can say, "I would rather be a doorman of the temple of my God than live in palaces of wickedness" (Ps 84:10, TLB).

We see ourselves now in an entirely new light. We see our lives as the residence of divine royalty. We are the temple, the abode, the habitation of the Most High. We are no longer kings in our own castles nor bosses of our own houses. We are but the doormen, the doorkeepers, whose responsibility it is to see that these temples shall not be desecrated, damaged, nor defiled.

This is the role of the priest. Peter, in his first epistle, chapter two, points out clearly that as God's royal priesthood, we have this honor and responsibility before our King.

If indeed the Kingdom of God is within me, then I shall make it my business to see that nothing enters there to harm or offend my Sovereign, the Spirit of the living God.

What I eat, what I drink will be checked with care. I shall not be a glutton nor a drunkard. I will not permit narcotics, drugs, stimulants, sedatives, nor other harmful materials to enter my body unnecessarily and thus pollute the temple of the Most High.

The same applies to my mind and emotions. I shall carefully monitor the material I read and the television shows I watch, lest my soul be distorted by the impressions received through my eyes.

Likewise the conversations I listen to, the music I hear, the programs I tune into by radio will be carefully scrutinized to see that no subversive material intrudes on the Kingdom of God within my mind and emotions and will.

Even in the realm of my feelings and sensory perception, nothing shall be touched, handled, or fondled that would lead to damaging imaginations or activities which could jeopardize this inner sanctuary of my King, the Christ.

In the area of my innermost mind, will, and spirit, I shall see to it that no subversive ideas, suggestions, attitudes, or human philosophies contrary to Christ's teachings and commands will infiltrate my life. The Kingdom of God is within me. It follows therefore that no fifth column of any sort, no traitor of any kind can be tolerated, which might undermine my loyalty or subvert my allegiance to my God.

These are very practical but very important considerations for the earnest Christian to consider. It is no use whatever to pray, "Thy kingdom come," unless we fully intend to cooperate with the establishment of God's government in our lives. It is facetious to pray this prayer unless we intend fully to do our part in seeing that His Kingdom within us is kept inviolate and undefiled.

When that Kingdom does come, when it is established, what are its chief attributes and characteristics?

Paul tells us very plainly in his letter to the church at Rome, "For the kingdom of God is not meat and drink; but righteousness, and peace, and joy in the Holy Ghost" (Ro 14:17).

In other words, the government of God within my life establishes an inner state in which righteousness, peace, and joy in a spiritual dimension dominate my days.

The Kingdom spoken of here is no outward, external empire of erratic emotions. Instead, it is an inner condition of mind, will, and spirit in which God's will becomes *my* will!

The righteousness referred to here is that state of right living which embraces attitudes, conduct, and relationships with God, others, and myself.

In the same way, the peace which we enjoy in God's Kingdom surpasses any sort of mere outward tranquility. It is that deep, delightful serenity of soul characteristic of God's presence. It is based upon being at peace with God, at peace with others, and at peace with ourselves.

Finally, the joy which is a hallmark of God's Kingdom is not a state of happiness dependent on changing circumstances or on what is *happening* around us. It is, rather, a serene, stable spirit known only to those who enjoy the presence of God's person within their lives. They sense and *know* that the King is in residence. In this awareness, there lies enormous assurance and quiet joy. They can be confident that, under Christ's control and through the guidance of His Spirit, their relationships with others, as well as themselves, can be free from fear and joyous with the strength of God, no matter how tempestuous life may be.

All of this is bound up in the coming of God's Kingdom into a man's life. The benefits are beyond our fondest hopes. They can be ours if, in utter sincerity and earnestness, we mean what we say in addressing our Father and requesting, "Thy kingdom come."

FIVE

Thy Will Be Done

"Thy will be done."

God's will. What is it?

Our Father's will. Can it be known?

The eternal will of the eternal God. Will it be done? Can it be carried out and complied with by mortal men? Does or can the will of God become of paramount importance to strong-willed, self-willed men?

All of these are very searching, serious questions. And they deserve—yes, much more—they demand, sincere and satisfying answers.

It is traditionally true to say that uncounted millions of men and women have repeated these four words without having the faintest idea what God's will is. It is even more sobering to reflect that even more people have repeated them without any intention whatever of seeing to it that our Father's will is done; even if they did know it. So in a sense there is much vain and pointless repetition of a phrase which actually bears enormous import for the Christian.

It is well to remind ourselves that this is the very practice which Christ had warned His disciples not to indulge in, just before He taught them His prayer. He said very plainly, "But when ye pray, use not vain

71

repetitions, as the heathen do: for they think that they shall be heard for their much speaking" (Mt 6:7).

What it amounts to is that most of us do not seriously consider what we are saying in repeating these words. We do not earnestly intend to have God's will done. It is a rather pleasant, pious sort of phrase that passes our lips too lightly.

Yet the tremendous truth is that the will of God and the doing of that will is the most important activity in all the world. The will of God is of such enormous magnitude and majesty that it completely overshadows all other concepts in the Christian life. Doing the Father's will is the one gigantic, central theme which should dominate the lives of all God's children.

That is why Jesus put it at the very heart and center of this prayer. It is the central theme about which all the others are grouped. It had been and was and ever would be the lodestar by which His own life was lived. What had He come down to earth for? To do the will of God. Why had He, the Son of God, set foot on the stage of human history? To do the will of God. Why did He condescend to be born among common men; to grow up among us as a man, a carpenter; to minister to us as a wandering prophet; to die deliberately for us, the sinless One for sinners; to be buried and rise again; to return to heaven? All of this was but to do the Father's will.

Again and again Jesus emphasized this fact during His earthly life. For example, in John 6:38, He states, "For I came down from heaven, not to do mine own will but the will of him that sent me."

In the garden of Gethsemane, where He faced the gigantic life-and-death decision of going to Calvary, the titanic struggle was resolved by the affirmation, "Not

my will, but thine be done." And only because, from
beginning to end, His life was lived fully in the context
of this concept could He be acclaimed and confirmed as
the Christ.

To make the subject of God, our Father's will, as
simple as possible, it is helpful first to realize what it is.
The will of God is simply God's intentions. It is what He
purposes. It is what He plans and wants to be done.

Obviously if this be so, it is quite apparent that He has
many wishes, intentions, desires, plans which He
would like to see fulfilled. Because He is God and because His interests are universal, it follows that His
wishes and His plans and His purposes run through and
into every area of the universe. Far too many people
assume rather naively that God's will is some spiritual
intent confined to a few cut-and-dried commands that
are found in Holy Writ. That the will of God is so vast, so
tremendous, so all-encompassing as to embrace all of
the universe as well as to permeate every detail of that
universe is beyond men's minds.

In order for us to fully appreciate the majesty and
magnitude of God's will, we must bring it out from
between the mere bindings of a book. We must see it
flowing free, running strongly through every segment
of heaven and earth. We must sense its power and impact made apparent everywhere, be it in the meticulous,
mathematical accuracy of the great stellar systems of
outer space; in the unbelievable forces within the nu-
cleus of an atom; in the fall of a fledgling from its nest; in
the response of a human will to the overtures of God's
own gracious Spirit speaking the reassuring words,
"[He is] not willing that any should perish, but that all
should come to repentance" (2 Pe 3:9).

God's will penetrates every area of life. It is apparent

in the orderly, physical laws and forces of the universe.
It is made real in all the biological systems of the natural
world. It is inherent in the vast complex chemical in-
teractions that control the organic and inorganic world.
This mighty will reveals itself in the beauty and wonder
of nature. It can be seen and sensed in all the exciting
environments of our planet. By far its most sublime and
remarkable demonstration was in the life of our Lord. It
carries on down through His family, the body of believers, the Church. It is found at work in any human heart
and character when a sincere soul seeks to know and do
the will of God. It is so all-pervading it even finds an
outlet in the details of day-to-day decisions which
Christ's followers make for His sake.

If we are to understand and appreciate the significance of this divine will, then we must, of necessity,
know something of the Author and owner of that will. It
is not possible to divorce or separate the will of God
from God Himself. His will is not something detached
from and external to the Person and character of our
Father in heaven.

On the surface this may seem obvious. Yet, it is surprising how many of God's children speak of their
Father's will as though it was something quite apart
from Him. They often act as if the will of God was merely
an abstract edict which could be acknowledged or ig-
nored at a whim. The fact of the matter is that to recognize and acknowledge His will is to recognize and acknowledge Him. To ignore and repudiate His will is to
ignore and repudiate Him.

This is so by virtue of the fact that God is not an
abstract idea. He is not an influence or an ethic. He is a
Person with all the attributes of personality which make

up a total person. And of this complete person the most important part is His will.

God, our Father, has a mind. He reasons. He thinks. "Come now, and let us reason together," He invites us in Isaiah 1:18. "I know the thoughts which I think toward you" (Jer 29:11). "My thoughts are not your thoughts" (Is 55:8-9).

Our heavenly Father has emotions. He feels. He senses. "For God so loved the world" (Jn 3:16). He is "touched with the feelings of our infirmities" (Heb 4:15). "As a father pitieth his children, so the LORD pitieth them that fear him" (Ps 103:13).

And, likewise, He has a will. With it He decides. He chooses. He purposes and plans. "I have chosen thee, saith the LORD of hosts" (Hag 2:23). "He hath chosen us in him before the foundation of the world" (Eph 1:4).

It is the onward progress and movement of these various aspects of God's total Person which demonstrate and so convince us of His character. And as was shown in the chapter dealing with His name, it is His character which is His glory, and, conversely, His glory lies in His impeccable character. This character is of such a superb caliber that it invites our total trust and solicits our wholehearted cooperation. It is essentially what validates our faith. It confirms our confidence in Him. This is why no matter how feeble or frail or infinitesimal our kernel of faith in God may be, because it has as its object the Person and character of our Father in heaven, its potential is unlimited.

Therefore it should be apparent to us that, if our confidence is in the person and character of God, it must be likewise in His will. There should be no doubt in our innermost being that, if God is good, if He is reasonable, if He is compassionate, then His will too is of the same quality and character.

Still it is surprising—much more—it is astounding, how many people profess to love God but fear His will. They claim to trust Him yet at the same time react against His will. One who does this finds himself in a hopeless impasse. It would be impossible to pray somewhat like this: "Our Father in heaven, hallowed be Your name; Your kingdom come; may Your will *not* be done."

It is an absurdity, but many endeavor to live this way.

Because of who God is, because of what He is like, because of the beauty of His behavior, because of the unique caliber of His character, His will is bound to be good and beneficial and acceptable, so that when we accept Him and sense our sonship, we also become clearly aware of His goodwill toward us in every aspect of life.

Fortunately for us, the will of God has found expression in both His work and in His words. It has been made clear to us not only in what He has done and still does, but also in what He said and still says. It is a most unfair charge to claim that God's will cannot be known. The truth is that most of us deliberately choose (with our wills) not to know. There is something very humbling about recognizing and acknowledging the magnitude of God's will. It tends to put the colossal conceit and intellectual pride of self-willed men into proper perspective, and, for this reason, most men reject it. They do not wish to acknowledge the will of God in the universe, much less accept the idea that it should be done at all in any area of their personal lives.

The will of God found its ultimate creative realization in producing the race of men. It was His intention to have beings resembling Himself, with an amazing capacity to accept and reciprocate His affection of their own free will. That such a relationship did not long endure without being shattered by man's self-will was and is no reflection on His good intentions toward us. That His very being yearned for objects of His love is evidence enough that His will for us from before the creation of the earth was of gracious and generous proportions.

The will of God, despite man's deceitful character, perverse personality, and strong-willed waywardness, continued to work for man's redemption, for his restoration to the family of God, for his rebirth and renewal as children of God. So much so was this the case, that, in accordance with His own will and His own wishes, He had His Son take upon Himself the form of a man and came to live among us, clothed in the human personality of Jesus Christ.

Jesus Himself endorsed and affirmed this concept when He stated emphatically, "I must work the works of him that sent me" (Jn 9:4). He was fulfilling in human form the very activity and attitudes that comprised His Father's will. From His earliest boyhood to the moment of His triumphal return to His Father's right hand, His entire earthly sojourn was simply doing His Father's will.

Nor did the outworking of God's will on earth end with Christ's return to glory. It has continued on down through the long centuries since by the working of God's Holy Spirit in the Church and in men's hearts and lives. This is how it is being done.

The will of God for this planet, for its people, for all that is contained in the expression, "heaven and earth," is yet to be consummated. For instance, in Ephesians

1:9-10, we read this inspiring statement: "For God has allowed us to know the secret of His plan, and it is this: He purposes in His sovereign will that all human history shall be consummated in Christ, that everything that exists in Heaven or earth shall find its perfection and fulfillment in him" (Phillips).

Other passages make it clear that the ongoing of God's will, ultimately, will result in the millennial kingdom and the creation of a new heaven and a new earth of such a quality that nothing we now know can be compared to it. It will enjoy such perfection, peace, plenty, as to completely outdazzle even our most fantastic hopes.

Then there is that second great half of the will of God that has found expression in words. Our Father's will has been articulated for us in human language. It has been passed down to us in a unique and very wondrous disclosure of what His intentions are toward us and for us. Through His written word, we can obtain very clear and explicit concepts of what He wants. And, in large measure, it is from this source that we derive very definite instructions on what He expects of us as His own children. This applies to every area of our lives, be it physical, moral, spiritual, or even in our careers.

It is often mistakenly thought that the will of God, as expressed in the Ten Commandments of Exodus 20, constitute His entire code of conduct for our lives. This is not so. For example, there are numerous passages throughout the Bible which give us clear and explicit instructions about such everyday matters as what we should eat; what we should drink; how we should think; how we should exercise; how we should work; how we should handle our money; how we should treat our wives, husbands, children, and parents. We are even instructed on such subjects as law and order, paying taxes, borrowing and lending, debts, hospitality, talking too much, as well as beneficial and wholesome sex.

Naturally it follows, does it not, that if we are going to know the will of God in such everyday affairs, we are going to have to read the Book in which that will has been laid out. Many of us neglect to read God's Word. Little wonder then that we are often so very ignorant of what He expects of us and what He has in mind for our own best interests.

The last statement is so important it needs to be examined carefully. God, our Father, being our Father and our God who loves us with enormous compassion and concern, bears infinite goodwill toward us. Because of this, all those guidelines laid down for our conduct and which constitute His will for us, have our own best interests in mind. His laws, ordinances, instructions, commandments, teachings are not those of a despot or tyrant who is trying to make things tough or difficult for us. They are rather His formula for successful and satisfactory living. And when we see this, we are bound to agree with the beloved apostle when he wrote in his first epistle, "For this is the love of God, that we keep [or carry out] his commandments: and his commandments are not grievous" (1 Jn 5:3).

It is in the light of the above that we can look at God's will, not with fear and dismay, but delight. This is what the psalmist means when he says, "I will delight myself in thy commandments, which I have loved" (Ps 119:47).

The will of God is not restricted to purely spiritual matters in Scripture. It covers the entire range of all our human activities. And this is what makes the Bible such a blessed, practical Book for God's children. It is the final authority to which they can turn in their difficult decisions as well as for the ordinary conduct of day-to-day living.

God's will is very much concerned that the human body be properly fed, clothed, exercised, regulated, rested, and kept clean. God's will is very much concerned with the simple fundamentals of wholesome houses, clean streets, well-kept farms, honest businesses, and the wise use of our natural resources. It permeates and penetrates every part of our physical world. And it is double-talk of the worst sort if we claim to be doing God's will in our spirits while we behave like beasts in our bodies.

Our Father's will is also very much concerned with our minds and emotions and our wills. There is a great mass of material in Scripture that deals with our moral conduct. As indicated earlier, this is by no means confined to the Ten Commandments. There is in the Old Testament alone an enormous fund of divine wisdom and instruction for any seeking soul. The Psalms pulse with divine light that can illuminate any person's path. The book of Proverbs is packed with more wisdom and common sense for successful living than any other piece of literature extant. In the four gospels of the New Testament, we find concentrated God's loftiest principles and most pungent teaching expressed in simple language by our Lord and Master, Jesus Christ. The Sermon on the Mount towers in glowing grandeur far above any other ethic ever propounded upon the planet. It is the will of God for the character and conduct of His people. Then on through the remainder of the New Testament, in a variety of histories, epistles, doctrinal treatises, and documents, we find the will of God for men's moral and spiritual life made very clear. Our business is to get into all this material and find out for ourselves what God says.

At this point it is well to pause a moment. It is not enough just to get in and study God's Word. It is not enough just to know what the will of God is. One then has to comply with it.

Jesus, at the very end of His Sermon on the Mount made this point with enormous emphasis. He said, "Not every one that saith unto me, Lord, Lord, shall enter into the kingdom of heaven, but he that doeth the will of my Father which is in heaven" (Mt 7:21).

It has been said, and rightly so, that no man or woman can possibly live up to the lofty standards of moral character and moral conduct set by our Saviour. That is to say no one can meet these demands in his own strength by virtue of self-will, steel-like resolutions, or constant vigilance. But a way and a means of practical application to our lives has been supplied by our Father. He did not give expression to His will merely to mock us. He does not indulge in sadistic exercises. He finds no fun in our failure to fulfill His expectations of us.

In the person of Christ Jesus, He demonstrated that One so imbued and indwelt by His own Holy Spirit could indeed live such a faultless life. And now that Christ has ascended to sit at His right hand, having Himself fulfilled all the will of God, His same gracious Holy Spirit, who indwelt Him, indwells our bodies and energizes us to do God's will. But, this is only on the condition that we will cooperate with Him.

Paul, in his epistle to the Philippian church, makes this very clear. "Let this mind [attitude] be in you which was also in Christ Jesus. . . .For it is God [by His Spirit] who worketh in you both to will and to do of his good pleasure" (Phil 2:5, 13).

There lies the secret: complete cooperation between my will and God's will.

As we progress in our desire to do all of God's will, it comes as a real surprise for some of us to find that our Father's will concerns the common round of our careers. He is very interested in what courses I shall study at school, what major I shall follow in college, which young man or lady I shall marry, which company I shall work for, what kind of car I will buy, which city or town I shall live in, what church I shall attend, how many children I shall have in my family, what sort of house I shall purchase, how my home shall be furnished, what clubs or societies I shall join, what friends or strangers I shall have in my home, what service I shall undertake to assist His people and thus benefit my community, what endeavors I shall make to be an uplift and inspiration to my generation.

There will steal over me, as I mature in my Christian life and outlook, an acute awareness that all I have and own or acquire has only been entrusted to me by my Father for the few years that my life lasts on this planet. My mind, my personality, my peculiar abilities, my physical strength and energy, my unique talents are not of my own making or manufacture. The idea of "a self-made man" is utter nonsense and colossal conceit. It is simply that some have applied their God-given talents in such a way as to have prospered. So when we see that, in essence, everything we have or acquire really does originate with God our Father, a feeling of direct responsibility to Him for its use will develop in our thinking.

This concept of being those who hold in trust all that they possess can be a most powerful force in helping us to do God's will. We will consider it very essential to see

that our time, our talents, our temperaments, our things
(possessions of all kinds), our tireless energy, shall be
used in accordance with His will and intentions for
them. We are not entrusted with these benefits just to
spend them on our own selfish interests. They have
been entrusted to us to bless our generation.

It is one thing to become acutely conscious of all this.
It is another thing to discover, day after day, just what
God's will is in the particular issues or decisions that we
must make concerning our careers. Many of God's children become very confused over deciding what is God's
will in very practical issues. Here are seven sure
guidelines to assist one in finding and doing God's will.

1. Is it definitely in agreement with God's will expressed and written in His Word? If so, fine. If not,
   don't do it.
2. Have you faced a similar situation before? If so what
   did God show you as His will then? If you made a
   mistake, don't repeat it.
3. If the decision is difficult and far beyond you, seek
   the wise and prayerful counsel of mature and godly
   persons who have the mind of Christ and know how
   to ascertain God's will.
4. Make the matter one of quiet but earnest prayer. Ask
   God, your Father, by His Spirit, to impress upon you
   distinctly by a deep inner conviction what the proper
   course of action is.
5. Our Father has endowed us with a fund of wholesome and practical knowledge which He expects us
   to use. We ignore it with risk.
6. Expect and wait to see events and circumstances
   surrounding this situation alter in such a manner as
   to influence your mind and will in determining

God's will. Time takes care of many decisions. We are prone to be too impatient and hasty. God is seldom in a great rush about things.

7. Anticipate that as time goes on, the way will either open or the way will close for you to proceed along any given course. This should be accompanied by a sense of acceptance, gladness that you are being made aware of God's will, happiness in doing it, and peace about it.

When these points are followed precisely, and there is no great conflict between them, one can be assured of knowing and doing God's will.

There are times when one must, of absolute necessity, make an almost instant decision. If the mind is divided and no clear guidance is immediately available, there is a helpful way to arrive at a choice.

With an open mind, ask God to guide unmistakably in listing the pros and cons on a divided sheet of paper. Being utterly honest before the Lord, ascribe three points to each reason—pro or con—of major importance. Ascribe two points to each reason of moderate importance. And give only one point to each reason of only minor importance. Then total up the figures. It will sometimes astonish one how overwhelming the evidence is for or against a decision. If one is as honest and objective as possible before God in this, it is proper to feel at peace about the outcome.

In closing this important chapter, let it be emphasized that if any man or woman is really eager to know and willing to do God's will, he or she may be completely confident that he will not be mocked. God's distinct will most assuredly will be made known to him or her. And, equally wonderful, by His own indwelling Spirit, that person will be given the courage and ability to comply with that will in joyous and full-hearted cooperation.

"Father, Thy will be done. Amen. So be it!"

SIX

In Earth, as It Is in Heaven

"In earth, as it is in heaven."

In the preceding chapter, we dealt primarily with what the will of God is. Its titanic proportions have been described. Emphasis has been placed on how this great will penetrates and permeates every part of the universe. It has been pointed out how tremendously important it is for us as God's people to see that His will is done.

But the basic question, and the one over which most of us mortals stumble is, "How?" *How* can the will of our Father really be done in earth as it is in heaven? *How* can His desires, His wishes, His intentions be realized on an earth dominated by evil; held under the tyranny of Satan; and populated by stubborn, self-willed men? Is it essentially possible? Can the divine desires and wishes of my heavenly Father really be fulfilled in me, at least, in this bit of human clay, in this small fragment of the earth?

Our Lord was not a deluded idealist. He did not indulge in idle speculation or empty dreaming. Nor did He pray impossible prayers. So when He said, "Thy will be done in earth, as it is in heaven," He did not envisage

87

that the will of His Father would or could be done in the hearts and lives of those who rejected His authority. It would be absurd to ask or expect that the will of God be carried out by those who were in no way in harmony with God.

But this did not mean that God's overall purposes for the planet would not eventually be realized. They will. In spite of men and nations set against Him, the sovereign intentions of the Almighty are bound to be achieved.

"Why do the heathen rage, and the people imagine a vain thing? The kings of the earth set themselves, and the rulers take counsel together, against the LORD, and against his anointed, saying, Let us break their bands asunder, and cast away their cords from us. He that sitteth in the heavens shall laugh: the LORD shall have them in derision" (Ps 2:1-4).

Yet, here, in this simple request, the thought is, "Heavenly Father, may Your will be done in this bit of earth, *in me* here and now, just as it will be done some-day on this earth."

This would be very simple, very straightforward, very feasible if we human beings did not have a will of our own. This is the single greatest deterrent to the accomplishment of God's will. We are not puppets who jump up and down, whirl our arms, or swing our legs by the pull of a string. Instead we deliberately make our own choices and reach our own decisions. We carry out our own ideas in response to our own wills.

Consequently we find ourselves faced by the fact that there are two wills moving separately, sometimes in harmony, sometimes in confrontation: God's will and my will. And the Christian's primary responsibility is to see to it that his human will responds to and complies with that of his heavenly Father. Well over 90% of all Christian growth and maturity and holiness lies in achieving this end.

In fact, we find that those great saints of God who have learned to know and love Him best, not only come to the place where they did the will of God but actually enjoyed the will of God. This is important to realize, because in heaven it is no hardship to do God's will, but a joy. Likewise in my heart, if God's kingdom on earth is there, doing the will of God should be a delight and not a drudgery.

The sooner a child of God discovers the great delight of moving in harmony with the will of God, the sooner he has set his feet on the threshold of heaven. For it is in doing the will of God and responding to it positively that heaven actually does descend to this fragment of earth and becomes a reality within. Because of our strong self-assertion and stubborn, unyielding wills, some of us deprive ourselves for years of the quiet joys and serene satisfaction that can be the heritage of those who adjust themselves to God's wishes.

The Scriptures use a number of very graphic illustrations to convey to us the manner in which God, by His Spirit, endeavors to manipulate and mold the minds and wills of men and women. Of these perhaps the most picturesque is that of the potter at work at his wheel. The picture of how an insignificant, unyielding, rigid lump of earth can, through the application of the master craftsman's skill and loving care, be formed into a beautiful, useful piece of china comes through clearly to us.

I watched a primitive potter at work in Pakistan. Nothing I had ever been told ever revealed to me half so clearly exactly what is meant by the phrase, "Thy will be done in earth as it is in heaven."

This aged craftsman, with deeply lined face, stooped shoulders and delicate, sensitive hands, welcomed my missionary companion and me to his little shabby shop on a back street of Peshwar. This trading town in the far northwest corner of West Pakistan stands in the foothills of the fabled Khyber Pass. It is a region as colorful as its notorious Phathan people. Up and down the dusty streets outside the potter's house roamed sharp-eyed, bearded, rifle-bearing tribesmen, bent on trade and barter.

Inside the shop the words from Jeremiah 18:2 came home to me clearly: "Arise, and go down to the potter's house, and there I will cause thee to hear my words."

In sincerity and earnestness I asked the old master craftsman to show me every step in the creation of a masterpiece. My request seemed to thrill him. As a small lad he had been apprenticed to a master potter in China who taught him every trick in the trade. Now he was happy to show me the skill and artistry that had been acquired through his long life working with clay. On his shelves stood gleaming goblets, lovely vases, and exquisite bowls of breathtaking beauty.

Then, crooking a bony finger toward me, he led the way to a small, dark, closed shed at the back of his shop. When he opened its rickety door, a repulsive, overpowering stench of decaying matter engulfed me. For a moment I stepped back from the edge of the gaping dark pit in the floor of the shed. "This is where the work begins!" he said, kneeling down beside the black, nauseating hole. With his long, thin arm, he reached down into the darkness. His slim, skilled fingers felt around amid the lumpy clay, searching for a fragment of material exactly suited to his task.

"I add special kinds of grass to the mud," he remarked. "As it rots and decays, its organic content increases the colloidal quality of the clay. Then it sticks together better." Finally his knowing hands brought up a lump of dark mud from the horrible pit where the clay had been tramped and mixed for hours by his hard, bony feet.

With tremendous impact the first verses from Psalm 40 came to my heart. In a new and suddenly illuminating way I saw what the psalmist meant when he wrote long ago, "I waited patiently for the LORD, and he inclined unto me, and heard my cry. He brought me up also out of an horrible pit, out of the miry clay." As carefully as the potter selected his clay, so God used special care in choosing me.

As the potter gently patted the ugly lump of mud in his hands into a round ball of earth, I knew God was dealing very plainly with my earthy heart. Gently the old man closed the door to the pit. He walked, clay in hand, over to where a huge, round slab of stone stood in the center of his shop. With meticulous precision, he placed the lump of earth exactly in the center of his wheel. The care he took in this apparently simple step astounded me. But it was necessary before he set the stone in motion with the clay whirling at its center.

Again the word of the Lord came through clearly to my heart from Psalm 40:2, "[He] set my feet upon a rock, and established my goings."

Just as the potter took special pains to center the clay on the stone wheel, so God exercises very particular care in centering my life in Christ. This was not a task that could be done down in the clay pit. I had to be literally lifted out of the horrible hole of my old, obnoxious life to be centered in Him who alone could set me going in a new direction. And the stone upon which I was placed was none other than Christ Himself, the Rock of God. I had never realized this before. Perhaps this was because of the darkness and despair of my former life. Yet now I saw it in amazing clarity. I too was a bit of earth in the Master's hands, and He was at work molding my life.

When the old potter settled himself on his wobbly little wooden stool before the stone, something impressed me enormously. It was the peculiar, fascinating look that crept across his lined face. A new light filled his eyes. Somehow I could sense that in the crude, shapeless fragment of earth between his hands, he already saw a vase or goblet of exquisite form and beauty. There was in this clod of crude clay enormous possibilities! The very thought seemed to thrill him. Out of this bit of mud would emerge a unique bit of beauty as his will was impressed upon it. His intentions, his wishes, his purposes for it were that it might become a handsome, useful article, like those other pieces of beautiful china that adorned his shelves.

And God's gentle Spirit spoke to me softly but surely in that dimly lit little shop, saying, "Don't you see how much anticipation and excitement fills your Father's heart as He looks on you and holds you in His hands? If only His will can be done in your life—in this bit of earth—a bit of heaven can be produced in your life."

The old gentleman began to whirl the wheel gently. In fact, almost everything I saw him do that day was done tenderly with a touch of compassion. The great slab of granite, carved from the rough rock of the high Hindu Kush mountains behind his home, whirled quietly. It was operated by a very crude, treadle-like device that was moved by his feet, very much like our antique sewing machines.

As the stone gathered momentum, I was taken in

memory to Jeremiah 18:3. "Then I went down to the potter's house, and, behold, he wrought a work on the wheels."

But what stood out most before my mind at this point was the fact that beside the potter's stool, on either side of him, stood two basins of water. Not once did he touch the clay, now spinning swiftly at the center of the wheel, without first dipping his hands in the water. As he began to apply his delicate fingers and smooth palms to the mound of mud, it was always through the medium of the moisture of his hands. And it was fascinating to see how swiftly but surely the clay responded to the pressure applied to it through those moistened hands. Silently, smoothly, the form of a graceful goblet began to take shape beneath those hands. The water was the medium through which the master craftsman's will and wishes were being transmitted to the clay. His will actually was being done in earth.

For me this was a most moving demonstration of the simple, yet mysterious truth that my Father's will and wishes are expressed and transmitted to me through the water of His own Word. For though I may sense that He holds me in His own wondrous hands, and though I may be aware that those same strong, skilled hands are shaping my character and guiding my career, still His will and wishes are conveyed and transmitted to me always through the medium of His Word. It is the water of the Word—the expressed will of God—that finds fulfillment in fashioning me to His will.

Suddenly, as I watched, to my utter astonishment, I saw the stone stop. Why? I looked closely. The potter removed a small particle of grit from the goblet. His fingers had felt its resistance to his touch. He started the stone again. Quickly he smoothed the surface of the goblet. Then just as suddenly the stone stopped again. He removed another hard object—another tiny grain of sand—that left a scar in the side of the clay.

A look of anxiety and concern began to creep over the aged craftsman's face. His eyes began to hold a questioning look. Would the clay carry within it other particles of sand or grit or gravel that would resist his hands and wreck his work? Would all his finest intentions, highest hopes, and wonderful wishes come to nothing?

Suddenly he stopped the stone again. He pointed disconsolately to a deep, ragged gouge that cut and scarred the goblet's side. It was ruined beyond repair! In dismay he crushed it down beneath his hands, a formless mass of mud lying in a heap upon the stone.

"And the vessel that he made of clay was marred in the hand of the potter" (Jer 18:4). Seldom had any lesson come home to me with such tremendous clarity and force. Why was this rare and beautiful masterpiece ruined in the master's hands? Because he had run into resistance. It was like a thunderclap of truth bursting about me!

Why is my Father's will—His intention to turn out truly beautiful people—brought to nought again and again? Because of their resistance, because of their hardness. Why, despite His best efforts and endless patience with human beings, do they end up a disaster? Simply because they resist His will, they will not cooperate, they will not comply with His commands. His hands—those tender, gentle, gracious hands—are thwarted by our stubborn wills.

In dismay I turned to my missionary friend and asked him in a hoarse whisper, "What will the potter do now?" The question was passed on. Looking up at me through eyes now clouded and sad, he replied with a sorrowful shrug of his tired old shoulders, "Just make a crude finger bowl from the same lump."

The stone started to whirl again. Swiftly, deftly, and in short order a plain little finger bowl was shaped on the wheel. What might have been a rare and gorgeous goblet was now only a peasant's finger bowl. It was certainly second best. This was not the craftsman's first or finest intention, rather, just an afterthought. A bit of earth, a piece of clay that might have graced a nobleman's mansion was now destined to do menial service in some beggar's hovel.

And the word of God from Jeremiah came home to me like an arrow to its target: "So he [the potter—my God] made it again another vessel, as seemed good to the potter to make it" (Jer 18:4).

The sobering, searching, searing question I had to ask myself in the humble surroundings of that simple potter's shed was this: Am I going to be a piece of fine china or just a finger bowl? Is my life going to be a gorgeous goblet fit to hold the fine wine of God's very life from which others can drink and be refreshed? Or am I going to be just a crude finger bowl in which passersby will dabble their fingers briefly then pass on and forget all about it? It was one of the most solemn moments in all of my spiritual experiences.

"Father, thy will be done in earth [in clay], in me, as it is done in heaven."

Do I really mean this? Do I really want it? Do I really enjoy having it happen to me?

The old potter was not yet done with the little finger bowl. Reaching up beside him, he lifted a very fine thread, nearly as slender as a human hair, from a nail on the wall. He dipped it in the water beside him. Then, with it thoroughly soaked, he stretched it tight between his hands. With the bowl whirling rapidly on the stone, he drew the fine thread through the clay, cutting off the base of the bowl from the clay beneath. The separation was swift and smooth and sure.

"That is just like our lives," I mused to myself. We are separated, set aside unto good works. There comes a time when we must be cut off completely from the old ways, the old life, the old attitudes, the old habits. We are new creations in Christ, made and shaped by the will of God for special service.

Gently the craftsman stood up now and moved his stool away. Tenderly he lifted the new piece from the stone and carried it across the room to set it on a shelf. "It must rest there quite a while to cure," he explained. "Then after that it will be fired in my furnace to put the final touches to it." Slowly he crossed to the other side of his shed. Beckoning to me, he pointed through a small quartz window where I could see the fire glowing in his hot retort. "The fire gives the clay its gorgeous glaze that you see on my work here." He lifted a choice piece from its place of honor on the shelf. "It all takes time, much time, but it is worth it. My name and reputation as a master potter are at stake!"

Clearly now I could see why at times it was necessary for God to put me on the shelf. I could see why His will for me was to go through the fiery furnace of hardship. It all took time. It was all essential both for my beautification and for God's reputation. It was all part of having my Father's will done in this bit of earth.

From the foregoing illustration of the potter and the clay, it should be clear that the key to the success or failure of our fashioning under the Master's hands lies in how we respond to His touch.

Now if we look at this in a spiritual dimension we

discover that the degree to which we respond to or resist God is the degree to which we are willing to obey Him. Unfortunately obedience is a most unpopular theme today. We live in a period of history when it is fashionable and popular to resist all restraints. It matters not whether it be in the home, at school, on campuses, in industry, toward government, or even against God. *Rebellion, resistance, confrontation* are the catchwords of our time. So it is not the least surprising to find many who are simply unwilling to submit to the will of God. It is considered stupid and demeaning to do what our Father in heaven wishes us to do.

To obey and to cooperate means to subject or submit myself to someone else. It means to give in to another. It means to put another's will first. It means, in essence, to just do what another wishes me to do.

Because of our personal, perverse, powerful pride this is extremely hard for us to accept. To be asked to obey raises our resistance. We feel sure we are debasing ourselves. This goes against our ego; our selfish self-centeredness.

Yet in spite of all this resistance, the Word of God comes through clearly and with enormous emphasis. "Obey and live! Disobey and die!" "Obey and be blessed; disobey and meet disaster!" "Comply with My commands and find life abundant; ignore them and be cut off!"

Strange as it may seem, many Christians associate the thought of obedience and obeying with rigid legalism. It need not be so. In fact in God's Word and in God's view, obedience and love are so intimately intertwined that we cannot separate them. For the proof, the ultimate demonstration that I love another is to put that one's wishes first, before my own. It follows, therefore, that if I love my mate, my parents, my school, my country, my heavenly Father, their wishes and their desires will be first, and it will be my joy and delight to do what they ask.

I say it will be a joy because the act of my cooperation and obedience is evidence of my love, affection, and respect for them. For my part the pleasure given to them by my obedience will be a rich compensation for any inconvenience it may have cost me.

The net result is that instead of having a confrontation, I find myself receiving generous cooperation. Instead of being cursed with ill will, hostility, and bitterness, I find my life blessed with peace and goodwill and beautiful comradeship. Instead of frustration, tensions, and turmoil filling my days, I find myself moving in a new dimension of freedom and joy.

It is no wonder the psalmist sang, "I delight to do thy will, O my God; yea, thy law is within my heart" (Ps 40:8).

To love the will of God, to love the intentions and purposes of God our Father is to comply with Him and His wishes.

Jesus Himself emphasized and reemphasized this point over and over. For example, "If ye keep [obey] my commandments, ye shall abide in my love" (Jn 15:10). "Ye are my friends if ye do whatever I command you" (Jn 15:14). "If a man love me, he will keep my words" (Jn 14:23).

To love Him is to obey Him. To obey Him is to do His will. To do His will is to have a bit of heaven on earth!

Who is the person who enjoys and feels wondrously free in his home, among family and friends? It is the one who obeys, cooperates, and complies with their wishes. Who is the person who revels and rejoices in the laws and liberty of his land? The one who obeys, loves, and cooperates with its constitution. Who is the person who enjoys the companionship and benefit of belonging to our Father in heaven and His family? It is the person who obeys and cooperates with His will.

God's will carries within it all that has been set in motion for our welfare and benefit. He has our best interests at heart. So to do His will is really to do ourselves as well as Him a great favor.

If a person sets himself against the will of God, the result is a catastrophic confrontation. This leads to hostility. The hostility produces ill will. Ill will in turn breeds bitterness and hate. These, like an awful cancer in the character, can utterly ruin us. They will distort our spirits, damage our emotions, endanger the well-being of our bodies, and alienate our family and friends.

It is perfectly valid to assert that no man or woman can violate and resist the gracious will of God without in the end being broken by that will. God's eternal love and concern for us has been expressed in His own un-changeable goodwill. And any person who proposes to ignore or—even worse—to deliberately revolt against or resist that will, can be sure he will be shattered by its irresistible intent.

Perhaps by this time the reader may well ask, "How does one become obedient? How does one reach the place where he really wants to do God's will and enjoy it?"

There are several definite steps we can take in this direction.

We must see and grasp the reasonableness of it all. If this has happened and a genuine desire has been born, then we must set the will to do it. With the help of God we determine definitely to cooperate with God's purposes.

Having made this very determined and definite decision, we then ask God, by His gracious Holy Spirit, to invade and permeate our minds, wills, and emotions, especially our wills.

As we set ourselves to obey God, as we decide and in practice actually do what God asks us to do, we discover God's Spirit is indeed given to us (Ac 5:32).

It is the Spirit of God, at work in our wills, minds and emotions, who produces there both an increasing desire to obey and an enlarged power to obey.

"For it is God [by His Spirit] who worketh in you both to will and to do of his good pleasure" (Phil 2:13).

As we deliberately respond to the directions and instructions that come to us from God's own Spirit, speaking through His Word, we will find the energy and strength and courage to do what He asks of us.

The final result is to find ourselves in complete accord and harmony with the will of our Father in heaven. This is to experience joy, serenity, usefulness, worth, and enormous adventure in our walk with God as we move in accord with His plans and purposes on this planet.

This in essence is precisely what Christ had in mind when He instructed His disciples to pray, "Thy will be done in earth [in me] as it is in heaven."

What a joyous experience!

SEVEN

Give Us This Day Our Daily Bread

"Give us this day our daily bread."

Does it not seem strange that in the very center of this great prayer, our Lord should suddenly switch the emphasis from something as majestic as the will of God to a subject as earthy as bread?

But really this is just like Him.

You see, with Christ there really is nothing common. It is one of our human tendencies to tuck things away very tidily into little compartments. We call one thing sacred and another secular. We esteem some aspects of life very spiritual and very special, while others are considered quite simple and rather insignificant.

The fact of the matter is that anything touched by the presence of God has upon it sacred significance. This is why all through the Scriptures God's people are instructed to live their lives ever conscious of the abiding presence of Christ. When we do this, then even the most mundane objects or activities assume enormous import.

Brother Lawrence stated this idea very well when he wrote simply, "I can even pick up a straw from the ground and do it to the glory of God."

Therefore it should not surprise us unduly that Christ

should include in this great prayer a request for food. It is, after all, the very basis of our existence. This applies whether we are dealing with the physical or spiritual aspects of our lives. The two realms are really contiguous. But, because of our traditional thought patterns, they are here referred to separately and will be dealt with in this chapter in that way. Still we should see that eating nourishing bread can be as significant to us as feeding on food from heaven.

The provision of food for the life of man is discussed all through the Word of God. Initially God gave man all that was needed to support and sustain his life without working for it. But after the first couple deliberately defied God's instructions and willfully refused to cooperate with His will, this entire arrangement altered. The categorical statement made to Adam after he sinned was, "In the sweat of thy face shalt thou eat bread, till thou return unto the ground" (Gen 3:19). Or, as another translation puts it, "Thou shalt earn thy bread with the sweat of thy brow, until thou goest back into the ground from which thou wast taken" (Gen 3:19, Knox).

As the carpenter craftsman, working in Joseph's woodworking shop in Nazareth, Jesus knew all about this. He later had to support His widowed mother and young siblings by the strength of His muscles, skill of His hands, and sweat of His brow. Hacking and chopping, sawing and planing, shaping and fitting the tough, twisted olive wood and hard, heavy acacia timber that grew in Galilee was no child's play. It was back-breaking toil that turned trees into cattle yokes, plows, tables, and candlesticks, that He could sell for a few shekels to buy bread.

Why then did He dare to ask now that He be given bread? Was it not God's decree that man must earn his bread? Was it not part and parcel of the whole plan for man on the planet that if a man did not work he should not eat? (see 2 Th 3:8-12.) Could anyone feel exempt from this principle? It must have been a revolutionary concept to Christ's disciples. A little later on in this same discourse with them, He elaborates on this concept of working and worrying in our constant struggle to survive. We must examine it to see what He meant.

The principles are fairly plain and straightforward. Basically He teaches us that the natural resources of the earth are supplied for us by God our Father. They are more than adequate to meet our basic needs. Just as He provides for the wild birds and the wild flowers, so He has provided enough for us. In the same way that birds must search for their food, and that flowers must extend their leaves to the sun for sunlight, and their roots into the soil for moisture and nutrients, so we must expend ourselves. God does not drop grubs down the gullets of young birds nor does He give handouts to indolent people who simply sit in the shade and do nothing.

Also, He would have us understand that all the many resources put at our disposal are really gifts from God. In James 1:17 we are told, "Every good gift and every perfect gift is from above, and cometh down from the Father of lights." So, be it soil or sunshine, rain or rare elements in the earth, air or ammonia, plants or animals, whatever is essential for the production of food has its origin with our heavenly Father. It is He who has bestowed this bounty upon the earth. It is through His generosity that the supply is sustained, even in the face of our extravagance, waste, and selfish exploitation of the planet.

In view of these concepts, Christ then instructs us in very plain and simple language to stop worrying and fretting over the provision of bread. He assures us that our Father knows it is essential to our survival. He has made the bread available if we but do our part. And what is even more remarkable, He assures us that if, unlike Adam and Eve who refused to acknowledge the primacy of God's will, we do just that, seeking first and foremost to cooperate with our Father's wishes, our bread will indeed be supplied.

"Seek ye first the kingdom of God, and his righteousness, and all these things [bread included] shall be added unto you" (Mt 6:33).

Putting all this into rather simple layman's language, we might state it this way: Any man or woman prepared to put God's wishes first in life is bound to have bread.

From the foregoing it should be apparent that the corollary to being given bread is that a person be right with God. Only the one who puts God first in his life, who above all else desires to see God's will done on earth as it is in heaven, is entitled to ask God to give them bread.

This is an important point that many miss. Millions of people pray this prayer who never put God first in their affairs, who have no thought of doing God's will or even complying with His commands. Yet glibly and gladly, they will ask God to give them bread.

It is a mark of the generosity of God our Father that in spite of all this He still sends rain on the just and unjust, still supplies sufficient for saint and sinner, still maintains the plant life of a planet, the majority of whose population ignores Him.

But those of us who know Him as our Father, who sense His love and concern for us, come daily, not only asking in humility for our bread but deeply grateful for the food already supplied.

Perhaps it is natural for us to take our daily food for granted. Especially is this true in our modern technological age with its affluence and welfare governments. But for those of us old enough to recall the dreadful hunger of the depression years, daily bread is still a significant aspect of life for which we are glad to pray and give thanks. While for those of us who have had to live abroad where poverty, starvation, famine, begging, and horrible hunger are a way of life, this petition is full of meaning. For uncounted millions of men and women, there is no assurance whatever that there will be bread today, much less bread tomorrow. They may not have had bread yesterday or the day before that.

So another concept which was clearly in our Lord's heart and mind was that, as God's people, we should pray that all His children everywhere might have bread today. Of course most of us are so busy with our own lives, we are so preoccupied with padding our own nests and feeding our own already overstuffed stomachs that we really do not take time to care much about the hungry elsewhere.

It will be noted Jesus said, "Give us this day our daily bread." He did not say, "Give me all I can consume on myself." When He was among us as a man, it is deeply moving and touching to see His concern for the hungry crowds. And He did not spare either Himself or His disciples in seeing to it that they were properly fed.

One of the very practical ways in which we can help to make this prayer much more than just a pious platitude is in helping to share and distribute the bounty given to us with others. This is part of feeding the hungry and giving water to the thirsty, which Jesus pointed out to be of such importance in God's estimation.

In addition to the foregoing, we must, of course, realize that Christ's primary concern was not with the bread used only to sustain our physical frames. His outlook and approach to all of men's problems embraced the whole of man, his body, his mind, his spirit. And there was just as much need for man's soul and his spirit to be nourished daily as there was for his body metabolism to be maintained. As has been reiterated in God's Word, "Man shall not live by bread [grain bread] alone, but by every word that proceedeth out of the mouth of God" (Deu 8:3; Mt 4:4; Lk 4:4).

The amazing thing is that this statement was first made by Moses to a nation whom God had supplied with manna day after day, during all their years of wilderness wanderings. He was emphasizing that this remarkable provision for their purely physical needs was not sufficient to sustain them in soul and spirit.

What kind of hard, belligerent, brutish human beings most of us would be were we divested of food for our souls and refreshment for our minds. Any person long deprived of the uplift and inspiration of all that is noble, lofty, sublime, and worthy quickly degenerates to the savage state. So if we are going to be honest and practical in this prayer, we need to take advantage of the gifts afforded us each day for the nourishment and stimulation of our souls.

As essential as all the foregoing may be for the welfare of men, there can be little doubt that the thought uppermost in our Master's mind when He asked for daily bread, was that of spiritual nourishment. Of course this may seem obvious. The trouble is, most of us do not really pause to reflect when we repeat the prayer.

Is it not surprising that Christ should request bread, when He Himself asserted that He was the bread from heaven? (see Jn 6:32-58). Is it that He here teaches us the great fundamental truth that we must daily draw upon the very life of God, as He did? For, just as God our Father is the Author and giver of all temporal benefits bestowed upon us, so He is likewise the giver of spiritual sustenance. Jesus made this clear when He stated, "My Father giveth you the true bread from heaven" (Jn 6:32).

In this discussion about bread, there are several salient points which merit our attention if we are to understand why Christ included this petition in His prayer. First, like the manna of former times, it was something that was collected each day. Second, it was best when gathered early. Third, one day's supply could not be carried over for the next, except before the Sabbath. And last, it was a food that came from God.

Our Lord made it very clear that to come to Him was to eat spiritual bread. As with manna so with Him, we have to come regularly, daily, to derive nourishment afresh from God. To partake of His resurrection life is to feed on heavenly bread. In this way the hungry heart can be satisfied and filled.

There is a bit of mystery to all of this. Yet it is not really surprising, for, even at our best, we humans can scarcely grasp the unique and wondrous ways of God. In His mercy and generosity, He has used temporal concepts to explain spiritual truth so that our understanding of what is involved will be clear.

What is bread? It is the living kernels of grain, broken, crushed, bruised, and ground into fine flour. This flour is mixed with salt, water, and yeast. It is kneaded, shaped into loaves, then allowed to rise. After that, it is baked to a beautiful brown. In this new form as bread, the life of the grain provides life to those who eat it.

The life of the wheat is thus transmitted to man through the process of death and subsequent assimilation.

By a similar series of processes, the life of God in Christ has been made available to us. Our Saviour became God's grain. It was He who was broken and bruised at Calvary. He there took upon Himself our sins and ourselves. Out of that crushing, out of the grave, out of death itself, emerged the risen and resurrected One. He thus became God's bread for us.

Just as there is an enormous difference between bare kernels of grain and a loaf of bread, so there is a remarkable difference between Jesus of Nazareth and the risen Lord. The life of the wheat is limited to the kernel until it is crushed and milled. So the life of God in Christ was confined to His single earthly body until after His death and resurrection. Then He became available to all men everywhere by His Spirit. In this way, any man who hungers for bread from heaven, for life from God, for the vitality of Christ, may find Him available through His Spirit.

The special responsibility of the gracious Holy Spirit is to take the things of Christ, the life of Christ, the attributes of Christ, the character of Christ, and transmit them to us. This whole concept is made very clear to us in John's gospel, chapters 14-17. It is the actual resurrected life of Christ which is thus imparted to us. It is in this way that His life is made real in me and becomes part of my life. His life becomes my life.

With this then as a background, we can comprehend Christ as the bread from heaven. The prayer He taught us to pray becomes a most potent and powerful plea for the very life of God Himself. This is no mere, casual request for just ordinary food. It is a deep, desperate yearning to have the risen Christ made real in me each day. "Oh Father, give me this day my daily bread!" "Oh Father, let the very life of Your resurrected Son, my Lord the risen Christ, become my life today!"

Such a petition, such a prayer, such a desire could and does originate only with God Himself. It is not the sort of thing to spring from any self-centered, self-satisfied heart. Marvel of marvels, Christ Himself promised that anyone who so hungered would be filled (Mt 5-6).

If I, an ordinary mortal man, am nourished daily with the very life of Christ, what happens? Do I remain the same sort of person I was before I was given this bread from above? The answer is a very positive *no*.

There will gradually but surely steal over my life some amazing changes. My character will become like that of Christ Himself. My conduct will begin to resemble His conduct.

There will be formed in my mind the sort of thoughts that are in His mind—goodness, beauty, peace, and contentment. There will be born in me the same attitudes which He bears to others—compassion, acceptance, concern, and genuine forgiveness. There will be powerful and compelling motives produced within my being that have as their source the sort of love and understanding that He has in His heart.

The very life of the risen Lord will reach out through my hands in tenderness to actually touch the hands of those who suffer, to lift the load of the heavy laden, to mow a lawn for a friend, to dig a garden for a neighbor, to pen a letter to a lonely soul suffering awful boredom.

The life of Christ finding expression through my feet will take me to visit the sick, to carry some fruit or a bouquet of flowers to some stranger, to take time for a quiet walk with my mate or friends.

This life of Christ in me will find expression through my voice and lips and looks. It may be no more than a fleeting smile to a stranger, a gentle word of appreciation to someone who has served me in a store or restaurant, a few words of sincere endearment to those who are close to me. So, wherever I walk and wherever I live, there will be left behind a warm, uplifting legacy of goodwill.

This "daily bread" on which I feed will bring about subtle yet profound changes in my personal life-style. After all, it is Christ Himself who, by His Spirit, is permeating my whole being. Gradually I shall find myself less and less preoccupied with the sham and front, pretense and pretext of the secular scene. Pomp and pride and passion that command and demand so much of mortal men will no longer hold me in their grip. My foolish pride, my trivial vanity will be seen for the childish, self-centered characteristics that they are.

It has been said, "You are what you eat." If we feed our souls and spirits on God's bread from heaven, it follows that is what we shall become. This is a powerful principle. It explains why the Master included this apparently earthy petition in His noble prayer.

EIGHT

And Forgive Us Our Debts

"And forgive us our debts."

The second petition in the Lord's Prayer which deals with our human dilemma is, "And forgive us our debts." The first three requests relate to the role of God as our Father. The last four focus on our very human needs as God's children. Of these seven, the matter of forgiveness assumes such enormous importance that it is the only one which our Lord later took the time to reemphasize and develop in depth.

The thoughts and concepts held in the Master's mind when He said, "Forgive us our debts," were much wider than this simple petition implies. Evidence of this can be found in the various ways this has been rendered in different translations. Here are some examples:

"Forgive us our trespasses" (Knox).
"Forgive us our shortcomings" (Weymouth).
"Forgive us what we owe to you" (Phillips).
"Forgive us our sins" (TLB).
"Forgive us our resentments" (Amplified).
"Forgive us the wrong we have done" (NEB).

111

Several salient points stand out sharply in this petition and command our attention. When we recognize them, then this prayer becomes a most poignant plea, the deep heart cry of a truly contrite soul.

If we sincerely pray, "Forgive us our debts," or, "Forgive us our trespasses," then we are openly and candidly admitting ourselves to be guilty of wrongdoing. Now this really does not come home to many of us who repeat these five simple words. Thousands of dear people who recite the Lord's Prayer do not see themselves really as debtors, trespassers, sinners, or offenders. They do not consider themselves actually guilty before God.

And, of course, it follows, does it not, that it is not until one feels convicted of wrongdoing that there is any sense of need for forgiveness? The irony of it all is that uncounted people do feel quite innocent. Consequently this petition, instead of being a genuine desire rising from a penitent heart, is often little more than an empty repetition of words by a self-satisfied soul.

All of which leads to the second very searching concept. Do I indeed come to my heavenly Father as one who feels indebted to Him? Do I sense in some deep instinctive way that I have trespassed on His love and generosity? Am I acutely conscious of wrongdoing, of wrong attitudes, of wrong motives? Unless I am, then obviously this prayer is not only pointless but absurd.

In saying this I am not advocating nor even suggesting that as God's children we are to indulge in morbid introspection. It is neither wholesome nor beneficial for us to become preoccupied with our particular faults and failings. Rather, the overwhelming emphasis placed upon God's people all through Scripture is that we are reborn, recreated as new creations in Christ Jesus. We are urged to forget those things which are behind us and to press on to new and abundant achievements through the indwelling power and presence of God's own gracious Spirit within us (Phil 2:13).

Yet none of this nullifies the fact that we should come to our Father keenly sensitive to sin and selfishness in our lives. The very recognition and admission that we are debtors, and trespassers produces within the human heart a genuine humility that opens our whole being to the presence and Person of God Himself.

"The LORD is nigh unto them that are of a broken heart; and saveth such as be of a contrite spirit" (Ps 34:18).

Perhaps the next point it is well to remind ourselves of is that our petitions are not likely to be answered if we come in an attitude of arrogance and pride. If we entertain the haughty idea that we are not debtors or trespassers at all, then the likelihood of knowing forgiveness is remote indeed. "God resisteth the proud, but giveth grace unto the humble" (Ja 4:6).

No doubt the thought held uppermost in Christ's mind when He taught this prayer was that of a human heart coming humbly to seek restoration from a forgiving Father. After all, He Himself made it abundantly clear to us that God's attitude toward anyone who sought forgiveness was one of immediate reconciliation. God our Father never holds anyone at arm's length who shows the slightest inclination to turn toward Him in honest and open need of forgiveness.

Now, it may very well be asked, "But what if I don't feel I have done wrong? What if I don't feel in need of forgiveness? What if I don't sense my indebtedness?"

The only possible answer which can be given is that such a soul has never yet had a personal encounter with the living Christ. That one has never yet sensed the overwhelming love and concern of God for him as a Father for His child.

It is when we stand alone, quietly, earnestly contemplating the cost to God of our forgiveness made possible by the cross, that there floods over us our deep debt of love to Him. The cross stands central in our Father's magnanimous scheme for the forgiveness of all men of all time. Someone, somewhere always must pay the penalty for misconduct. He Himself undertook, at Calvary, to bear that cost, to absorb the penalty, to pay the enormous price for our sin.

"For God caused Christ, who Himself knew nothing of sin, actually to be sin for our sakes, so that in Christ we might be made good, with the goodness of God" (2 Co 5:21, Phillips).

The majesty and the mystery of this titanic transaction that took place on the cross is beyond our ability to fully grasp. Any person who pauses, even for a few moments, in serious contemplation of Calvary must be overwhelmed by the generosity of our Father God. Imagine, if you can, His anguish at the sight of His sinless Son, bearing our burden of sin, paying the penalty for our perverseness and pride, broken, bruised, His blood outflowing, for our forgiveness! Little marvel great darkness covered the entire earth during that cataclysmic event. Little wonder that Christ, who already knew and foresaw all of this, should include in this prayer, "Forgive us our debts."

The outstanding, eternal debt which all men of all time owe their heavenly Father is a debt of gratitude and of love for the price paid for our forgiveness. The cost of that forgiveness was Calvary. No man, no woman who contemplates this expression of our Father's love and concern for us can help but feel a deep sense of unworthiness.

It is in the white light of such overwhelming generosity and graciousness that the best of our behavior appears pretty tawdry. It is in the presence of the sublime Person and selfless love of our Lord, the Christ, that the loftiest of our inner attitudes look selfish. It is in the awareness of the amazing mercy and goodness of our God that the best we have to offer is the simple admission that we are debtors to the grace and love of Him who loves us with an everlasting love.

Any transgressions we have committed, any offenses for which we are responsible, any misdeeds we admit, are wrongs against the compassion and concern of our Father. To see this is to feel a deep need of His forgiveness. To sense this is to seek reconciliation with Him now and always.

It is no wonder, then, that Christ should include this request for forgiveness in His prayer. It is the key which unlocks the door whereby we enter a rich and wondrous relationship to God our Father.

We live in a world where men and women often feel deep down inside that something is basically missing from life, a sense that somehow they are out of touch with eternity. There is a foreboding that they have failed to find fulfillment. A strange, restless void that no human or material achievement can satisfy occupies the center of their beings. Deep down they know something is wrong, something is missing, but what?

So when Christ taught His disciples this prayer, this petition was included to cover and deal with this deep need in the human heart. As long as we sense in any way that sin or wrongdoing stands between us and God or between us and others, we feel estranged and apart. It is only the acute awareness that forgiveness has been fully granted which draws us to Him and to other human beings and makes us feel true fulfillment.

Many of the world's leading religions teach and admonish men to try to make amends for their misconduct. They urge their followers to pay penance or to achieve some sort of compensating merit by dint of good works or self-discipline. None of these succeed in setting the soul at peace, but, rather, they only plunge it deeper into despair.

Christ, however, comes to us quietly and invites us to simply admit that we are wrong within and in need of forgiveness. He makes no greater demand upon us than that of sincerely pocketing our pride and seeking simple reconciliation with our Father, who is so very fond of us and so very eager to extend His forgiveness to us the moment we seek it.

"Forgive us our debts" may well be the four most important words that ever cross our lips, provided we really mean them. Any man, any woman who comes to our Father in heaven with a genuine, heartfelt attitude of contrition is bound to find forgiveness. There will fall from the shoulders the old burden of guilt, and, in its place, there will be wrapped around our hearts a radiant sense of warmth, affection, love, and acceptance. "You are forgiven. You are mine. You do belong. You are home!"

This is the reception which the father gave the prodigal son when he came home asking forgiveness. Little did he realize, all the time he was away from his home and his father, that he was a forgiven man. Little did he know that, despite his misconduct, his father's love and concern for him had never diminished. Little did he recognize the yearning outreach of his father's heart toward him, even when his behavior besmirched and shamed the family name.

This is perhaps the most poignant picture portrayed for us in all of Scripture depicting the loving forgiveness of our Father. The son's forgiveness was not contingent upon a change of conduct or his making a fresh resolution to behave better, or even upon his sense of remorse and contrition. His forgiveness was freely bestowed and gladly given simply because he had come, willing to admit his wrong and accept pardon. The very character of God our Father can do no less than extend this sort of total and complete forgiveness to all who turn to Him for it.

Jesus knew all about this. He had been a resident of heaven for untold eons of time. Over and over again, He had shared in the ecstatic joy that swept through that celestial realm when even a single soul, searching for peace of heart and serenity of spirit, had simply turned to God and in sincerity prayed, "Forgive me my wrongdoing."

NINE

As We Forgive Our Debtors

"As we forgive our debtors."

In all of our Lord's Prayer, by far the most difficult phrase is, "As we forgive our debtors." It is not easy for us either to understand or to apply in a practical way to our daily living.

There has been enormous confusion about this part of the prayer. It has produced a great deal of discussion and many differing views down through the long centuries that the prayer has occupied such an important place in our Christian heritage.

For this reason it calls for our special attention. It is significant that newer translations of the New Testament put this passage into the past tense rather than the present. In other words, what Christ said, was this:

> Forgive us our debts, as we also
> have forgiven our debtors (RSV).
>
> or
>
> Forgive us the wrong we have done,
> as we have forgiven those who have
> wronged us (NEB).

And, of course, the question which immediately confronts us is, *have* we forgiven others who have wronged us? Do we really have a clear conscience in our relationship with other human beings? Is the atmosphere between me and my fellowman open and unclouded by hostilities? Do I still harbor old hates in my heart? Am I inclined to indulge in ill will over some hurt? Do I allow resentments to rankle beneath the surface of my life? Is there a gnawing grudge against someone tucked away secretly in the back of my memory? Is there a bitter root of recrimination buried deep down in my subconscious that sends up its shoot of cynicism to my conscious mind whenever I am reminded of some abuse or injustice I have suffered? Do the wrongs I have endured from others eat away inside me like a consuming cancer?

These are very probing questions. They get below the surface of the superficial attitudes with which so many attempt to accommodate themselves to the teachings of Christ.

It is probably safe to say that the overwhelming majority of men and women who repeat this prayer have not forgiven others. They have not written off the old debts. They do not have a clear conscience. A backlog of lingering ill will, hostilities, resentments, and animosities beclouds their relationship with others. They are still demanding restitution. They still insist on getting their pound of flesh.

How then can we come and in good conscience ask our Father in heaven to forgive us, when we have failed to forgive others? It cannot be done except very hypocritically. God sees right through this sort of sham.

Our Lord was always emphasizing the fact that our inner attitudes were more important than our outward actions. It was His assertion that our Father in heaven knew our attitudes and rated them far above our outward appearance.

Most of us from early infancy are conditioned to put on a brave front. We become exceedingly skilled at pretense. We are good actors. We can say one thing but think quite another. We can smile sweetly at someone yet hold hidden resentment against him down below the surface. In all of this we may be able to bluff other human beings, but we simply cannot get away with it in dealing with the searching Spirit of God our Father.

Consequently if we are going to repeat this prayer and hope for it to have an impact either on God or ourselves, the phony pretense and playacting have to end. We must become deadly serious in our statements. What we say must be in a spirit of sincerity and truthfulness.

"God is a Spirit; and they that worship him must worship him in spirit and in truth" (Jn 4:24).

If we cannot honestly say we have forgiven others or are unwilling to forgive them, we should find out why. And having seen the cause, do something at once to put matters right.

Why do most of us have trouble forgiving those who have wronged us? Why is it so hard to give up old resentments and ill will? Why do we harbor hate and grudges? Why do we allow bitterness, hostility, and antagonism to cripple our characters, twist our personalities, and blight our relationship to others? All of this leads to enormous tension, stress, and darkness within.

Many of us do not even realize that this state of affairs exists in our lives. In some cases we have lived this way so long we are scarcely aware of the warfare within ourselves. Belligerence, spite, and ill will have been companions whom we almost accept as normal life partners.

Beneath all our difficulties in forgiving others lies the

formidable foundational fact of human pride. The iron-like resistance of our egos, the great, central *I*, which stands like a huge, steel beam at the very core of our makeup refuses to budge, or bend, or be broken. We insist on our rights; we defend ourselves; we lay claim to our privileges; we hold fast to our positions. *Mine, me,* and *I* stand guard, jealously protecting our personal self-esteem and our proud reputation.

Picture an impregnable fortress, in which self sits upon the throne of the life. High walls of self-defense are built all around the personality. Anyone who dares to say or do anything which is provocative or threatening is considered a trespasser. Our immediate reaction is to lash out in retaliation or else quietly withdraw within the walls of self-defense. We pull up the drawbridge of open, friendly approach, holding others off at a cool arm's length.

All such self-esteem and self-preservation comes at a very high cost. It cuts us off from others. It turns us into self-centered, self-pitying introverts. It makes us hard, haughty, callous, quick to find fault, yet so very sensitive to our own hurts.

How can we get over this? What can change these inner attitudes that are so damaging, both to ourselves and others?

The answer lies again in coming to Christ and seeing something of what He endured for us at Calvary. Calvary stands eternally as God's demonstration to us of total selflessness. It towers above time as the supreme act of self-denial in a world that is largely selfish and self-indulgent.

It was no small thing that our Lord, who was God in human form, should be willing to humble Himself, make Himself of no reputation, take upon His innocent

Person our wrongs, pride, and perverseness. All of this He did without murmuring or complaining.

This is the exact opposite of our usual behavior. It is the difference between God's conduct and man's conduct. It is love in action as opposed to selfishness in attitude.

If Christ had insisted upon His rights, if He had been interested in maintaining only His reputation, if He had taken umbrage at every unfounded charge against Him, as we generally behave, there would have been no cross, no self-sacrifice on our behalf, no forgiveness of our faults, no reconciliation to God our Father!

It is no wonder, then, that Paul should write to the Christians at Ephesus, "Be ye kind one to another, tenderhearted, forgiving one another, even as God, for Christ's sake hath forgiven you" (Eph 4:32).

Dr. Martyn Lloyd-Jones, the great minister of London, wrote, "Whenever I see myself before God and realize something of what my blessed Lord has done for me at Calvary, I am ready to forgive anybody anything. I cannot withhold it. I do not even want to withhold it."

A second view we can get of Calvary is a very practical one. While our Saviour lay stretched prone upon the cross, with the spikes being pounded through His palms and ankles, He cried out a most incredible petition, "Father, forgive them; for they know not what they do" (Lk 23:34).

With that deep spiritual perception which was so uniquely His, He knew the heartless soldiers with hammers in hand did not know what they were doing. He knew that those who had flogged Him, taunted Him, betrayed Him, were not fully aware of what they were doing, much less why they did it.

Nothing else can so completely shatter self and crush

ego, leaving us undone, as a real look at our Lord at Calvary. In the presence of the Prince of peace dying upon the cross for me, my petty pride is pulverized. My self-esteem evaporates. The best I have appears as absolutely nothing. I see my sins and wrongs and misconduct for what they really are. I am then able to see myself in proper perspective, and, at that point, I am willing to forgive others.

The degree to which I am able and willing to forgive others is a clear indication of the extent to which I have personally experienced God my Father's forgiveness for me. The corollary to this is that anyone who is not willing to forgive another has certainly not known God's loving forgiveness.

A middle-aged rancher came to have coffee in our home one night. As the evening wore on, he unburdened his heart to us. For years and years, his life had been bleak and dark with a pent-up hostility against his harsh and overbearing father. In fact, at the last encounter they had had, the father, a huge, powerful man, had knocked him flat on his back. The younger man, though now a Christian, had never cleared the air between them.

When I pointed out to him all that Christ had suffered for his sake and how he in turn should be prepared to suffer humiliation in going to his father to put things right, it seemed a lot to ask. But that night he agreed he would do it.

Next morning early he went into the sagebrush hills alone and prayed for courage to go down and face his father. Then, swallowing his pride, he went to see the older gentleman. He told him of the deep hate and ill will that had accumulated in his heart against him. He told him how he regretted this. He told his father he was willing to forgive him all the abuse he had suffered at his hands, and in turn, asked to be forgiven for his own ill will.

The older man was completely overwhelmed. In a flood of joy, he flung his arms around his son and hugged him hard. It was the first time in thirty-four years the rancher could recall having felt his father's affection in this way.

A few weeks later this rancher and his father spent the whole day together, high in the hills, cutting special wood for the violins the father fashioned in his shop. I venture to say the quality of workmanship and the tone that comes from this old craftsman's instruments will, from now on, surpass anything he ever made before. There is a new music in his life. It is bound to be expressed in the violins he creates.

The beloved apostle, John, knew and fully understood this principle when he wrote to the early church, "If we confess our sins, he is faithful and just to forgive us our sins, and to cleanse us from all unrighteousness" (1 Jn 1:9).

Our Master put it like this: "If your brother wrongs you, go and have it out with him at once—just between the two of you. If he will listen to you, you have won him back as your brother" (Mt 18:15, Phillips).

It is the secret to contented relationships and good-will between human beings. What is more, it brings a smile of approval to our heavenly Father's face. He looks on and is satisfied.

It is in the bright light of understanding something of God's kindness that we in turn are able to extend genuine forgiveness and kindness to others. We are made willing to accept others as they are just as we desire our Father in heaven to accept us with all our weaknesses. The marvelous thing is He does. And wonder of wonders, we begin to discover that we too can accept and forgive others with all their faults.

This is to find rest from our own restlessness. It is to be set free from our fault-finding. It is to know a quietness of spirit not readily aroused by those who trespass against us.

TEN

And Lead Us Not into Temptation

"And lead us not into temptation."

At first thought, "And lead us not into temptation" appears to be a very simple petition. But is it?

Would God lead anyone into temptation? Any person who truly loves his Father in heaven does not wish to be tempted. We don't want to displease Him. Who wants to be dragged down into evil? We have no desire to do wrong, do we?

Surely God, our Father, knows this. Why then should He ever lead anyone into temptation? Does He do this? Does He place us in situations where we can or will be tempted?

As we contemplate this request, we begin to see that it really is not as simple as it seems. The questions that come to mind demand answers. Do we really understand the part played by temptation in a Christian's life? Do we know how to cope with it when it does come? Can we fully understand why we should ask our Father to keep us from it?

It is well for us to remind ourselves that when Jesus Christ taught His disciples this prayer, He Himself had already been through very severe temptation. We are told that after His baptism in the Jordan, "Then was Jesus led up of the Spirit into the wilderness to be tempted of the devil" (Mt 4:1).

It had been an agonizing, exacting ordeal from which He emerged totally triumphant. Yet it was a test of such magnitude that we read, "Angels came and ministered unto him" (Mt 4:11). After this conquest of His arch-enemy, He well knew temptation was a strenuous trial for anyone to face.

No doubt, then, one of the reasons He included this petition in the prayer was a compassionate concern for His followers. Being touched with the feeling of our infirmities, He shrank from seeing us exposed to the sort of temptation He Himself had endured.

One of the wondrous aspects of our Lord's temptations is the absolute finality with which He completely routed His tempter, that ancient adversary, Satan. There was simply no question of giving in. True, He could not sin, but, much more glorious, He *would* not sin!

The first Adam gave ground to Satan when tempted. Because of his defeat, sin entered into our human heritage.

The last Adam (Christ) gave no ground to Satan when tempted. Because of His complete victory in every encounter, righteousness is made available to those who follow in His footsteps, to those made members of God's family.

In spite of this, there lies within us the tendency to give way under temptation. Even at our best we are often beaten in our battles with the wicked one. Jesus knew this. It grieves Him deeply to see His followers succumb to Satan's skilled and cunning tactics.

When He knew Peter would be severely tempted to deny Him just before His crucifixion, He said to Peter,

"But I have prayed for you, that your faith might not fail." What solicitude!

He cautioned the eleven disciples who accompanied Him to the garden, with these words, "Watch and pray, that ye enter not into temptation; the spirit indeed is willing, but the flesh is weak" (Mt 26:41).

Basically, the above statement puts into very plain language the whole problem of temptation for God's children. If we are truly born into the family of God, we are bound to face not less but rather more temptation than before. The reason for this is that the enemy of our souls contests the control of our lives by God's gracious Spirit.

It is tremendously important to bear in mind that though temptation to evil is essentially a spiritual struggle that involves our wills, it is almost always fought in the realm of our personal passions (desires). This is why our Lord said that the spirit within us is willing to do what is in accordance with God's will, but it is our flesh, our personalities, our old natures, that buckle under in the battle for righteousness.

The temptations which assail God's children originate with Satan, called the great deceiver, and with our own lusts. Even the weakest Christian can sometimes rise to great heights of heroism in a cataclysmic hour of crisis. Instead Satan undertakes to get at us through our selfish, self-indulgent self-will. He tempts us to set our wills against our Father's will by appealing to one of three passionate points in our personalities.

These can be best understood and most easily set out in a diagram. It will be noted it was exactly along these lines Christ was tempted in the wilderness.

SATAN'S SUBTLE POINTS OF APPROACH
TO MY PERSON ARE THROUGH

1. MY EMOTIONS, i.e., self-pleasure, self-indulgence. Christ was tempted to make bread from stones.
2. MY MIND, my reason, i.e., self-preservation, self-reasoning. Christ was tempted to cast Himself off the Temple.
3. MY WILL, I, ego, i.e., self-prominence, self-assertion. Christ was tempted to accept an offer of world empires.

The devastating thing about these devilish tactics is that Satan generally chooses to tempt me in that area of my personality that is not yet under the full control of God's Spirit. He knows full well that I am much more likely to succumb to his inducements where he still can have sway over my person.

And the testing becomes a clear demonstration as to who really holds the upper hand in any given area of my life. Does God or does the devil? Consequently the whole contest for the child of God is one of deciding whether Christ, by His Spirit, controls me, or whether Satan, by means of my old self, manages me.

It is for this reason that Paul wrote so emphatically to the Galatians saying, "Walk in the Spirit, and ye shall not fulfill the lust [passions] of the flesh. For the flesh lusteth against the Spirit, and the Spirit against the flesh; and these are contrary the one to the other, so that ye cannot do the things that ye would" (Gal 5:16-17).

If perchance I find an area of my life in which I repeatedly succumb to temptation, it is because there *self,* my old passions, my old nature, my old desires, hold control rather than God's gracious Spirit.

It is for this reason that any man or woman who really desires to come completely under the control of God's Spirit must turn over all this territory to Him. Unless this is done as a deliberate act of the will, then that ground will be the beachhead from which the enemy will always launch another assault.

And to assert that it is God who allows this temptation to go on is to fail to understand the whole nature of temptation. James, in his usual very practical and pragmatic way, explains temptation this way: "Let no man say when he is tempted, I am tempted of God; for God cannot be tempted with evil, neither tempteth he any man; But every man is tempted, when he is drawn away of his own lust [passions], and enticed. Then when lust hath conceived, it bringeth forth sin; and sin, when it is finished, bringeth forth death" (Ja 1:13-15).

Our Master knew this. Because of the dire consequences attending any defeat in temptation, He urged us to pray that we might not be exposed to it.

I have sometimes wished this petition had a short rider attached to it this way, "And lead us not into temptation, but guide us by Your Spirit."

Of course, our Father does endeavor to do this. The problem is we are not always sensitive or responsive to the overtures of His gracious Spirit. We are not always prepared to give Him control of our conduct. We are not completely sure that He can manage our affairs. We are not always willing to choose His way. So, self reasserts itself, and wherever this happens the terrain is open for Satan to tempt us.

In almost every case where this does occur, it is not our loving Heavenly Father who has led us there. It is our own self-will. It is our own choice. The only exceptions are those instances in which God allows us to be tested and exposed to hardship in order to enlarge our confidence in Himself. For it is there He demonstrates to us His amazing ability to deliver us triumphant out of the temptation. Our faith in His faithfulness is fortified. And our characters are conformed to His.

Also it is well to remind ourselves, always, that He does not allow us to be tempted above or beyond that which we are able to endure or bear. (1 Co 10:13; Heb 2:18).

There is often confusion and deep disquiet, especially among new Christians who find themselves being tempted. Very often they feel that the inclination to do wrong is in itself evil. This is not so. To be tempted is not to sin. To give ground to the enemy and allow him to control us, contrary to the will and purpose of our Father, is to sin.

There are six steps which follow one upon another that lead to defeat in temptation.

The first step in temptation is often the least obvious. We are given a false impression by Satan that whatever wrong we do really is not serious. Somehow, in very subtle ways, he convinces us that self-will and self-centeredness in counteraction to our Father's will are not crucial matters. "After all," he hints, "is God your Father not loving and forgiving and merciful? What harm is done if you do slip a bit and give ground?"

Second, Satan makes us see (either in fact, or in our minds) something, someone, or some situation which he is sure will appeal to our self life. In other words, he presents a picture to us that arouses some passion or desire in our personality.

Third, this produces, unless we understand his tactics, a powerful response within us. A deep and compelling desire is actively aroused. Often it appears very pleasant or very reasonable or very much to our personal advantage to pursue it.

Fourth, we begin to toy with this idea. We entertain it.

We play with it. It appeals increasingly; so we finally reach out to take it. At this point, we have actually fallen for Satan's ruse and given ground. Here we sin against God!

But the action is not over. Temptation, once succumbed to, has dire consequences. We have become a slave to sin and Satan. We are now under his orders in this area.

Fifth, we proceed to act on that which was presented to us in such a subtle, skillfull manner. But the moment we do, we are chagrined and dismayed by our own defeat. We become downcast and discouraged. The devil is delighted!

The sixth and final step is to hide the defeat. We attempt to excuse or conceal the debacle from others and from God. This cuts us off from open communication with our Father. At this point a sense of deep despair and sin and separation overwhelms us.

A careful examination of the sequence of events in Adam and Eve's temptation will show these six steps in action.

1. Satan led them to believe that eating the forbidden fruit would not really have serious consequences (Gen 3:4).
2. Satan presented the picture of them becoming as gods, knowing good and evil, if they ate the forbidden fruit (Gen 3:4-5).
3. This had a tremendous appeal. It aroused the desire to become great and wise. It seemed pleasant and reasonable (Gen 3:6).
4. They actually reached out and took the fruit. They accepted it. They ate it. They took it right in. This

was self-will exerted against God's will. This was sin (Gen 3:6).

5. The result was they sensed at once that they had been taken in. They were stripped. They were victimized. They stood naked and ashamed. They were embarrassed and chagrined (Gen 3:7).

6. They attempted to hide from their heavenly Father. They were cut off from open, frank, honest communication with Him (Gen 3:8).

When God came to meet with them, they were in despair, endeavoring to hide from Him. He called out, "Where are you?" Not that He did not know. He did! Here, for the first time, a son of God had succumbed to Satan's tactics. Now he was estranged from his Father. Did Adam know this? "Do you know where you are, Adam?" is really what God was asking.

Do we know where we are when defeated?

Without question, it is because of this sequence in our temptations, leading to estrangement from our Father, that Christ prayed, "Lead us not into temptation." We don't want to be separated from Him who loves us so much. We don't want to walk at a distance. We don't want to be His discouraged, defeated children.

Fortunately we are not left without definite tactics to counter temptation. We are given explicit instructions on how to handle it. And the steps to victory in this field are every bit as clear as those which lead to capitulation and defeat. These will be dealt with in detail in the next chapter.

At this point, one thing should be made very clear. Temptation in itself is not necessarily an evil experience. It is part and parcel of our Father's plan for producing people of strong character and Christlike qualities. When He created us as freewill beings, He knew we would be confronted with never ending choices for good or evil. Our characters as His children are the sum total of the choices we make in a life fraught with temptation. Temptation, from God's standpoint, is our great testing ground. It is the disciplining we undergo as we mature. It can help us grow up into godliness under the guidance of His gracious Spirit.

Dr. J. B. Phillips, in his splendid translation of James 1:2-4, makes this very clear to us.

"When all kinds of trials and temptations crowd into your lives, my brothers, don't resent them as intruders, but welcome them as friends! Realize that they come to test your faith and to produce in you the quality of endurance. But let the process go on until that endurance is fully developed, and you will find you have become men of mature character with the right sort of independence."

Precisely the same sort of view is fully developed in Hebrews 12:1-17.

The picture of temptation presented to us all through Scripture is that it is not an easy ordeal. It is something most of us would prefer to avoid. It is an integral part of the Christian's life. It is something we are to accept as a challenge. We can use it to demonstrate, as did our Lord, that we are determined, with His help, to do God's will. It is an opportunity for us to prove both to ourselves and to a skeptical world, "Greater is he that is in you, than he that is in the world!" (1 Jn 4:4).

It is perfectly proper and legitimate for us to ask our Father in heaven not to lead us into temptation, simply because we know our hearts and their natural propensity to evil. Still, He has made provision for us to be triumphant in temptation. He is able to deliver us from

evil. The decision as to whether or not we shall triumph
in temptation is pretty much ours.

This is a sobering thought. It shows how much our
Father believes in us. He is convinced that if His Son,
Christ our Saviour, could overcome, so can we! Bless
His name.

ELEVEN

But Deliver Us from Evil

"But deliver us from evil."

In various translations, this phrase is rendered, "But deliver us from the evil one," or, "Save us from the evil one."

As we saw in the chapter on temptation, the Christian's conflict is essentially a contest with the evil one. It is not just a question of coping with sin or self but rather a matter of being tempted by Satan through our self and its natural inclination to sin.

There is a tendency for us to think of sin, self (or self-will), and Satan as being more or less widely separated from each other. In fact the three are so closely intertwined that they cannot be readily divorced from each other. Or, to put it another way, what it really amounts to is Satan, appealing to self (our self-will), uses it as a means to make us sin. He influences us to exert our wills in contradiction to the expressed will of our heavenly Father. This is to sin.

Because of this, Christ taught us to pray emphatically, "Deliver us from evil [from the evil one]."

It is tremendously encouraging for us to know that this petition can be answered positively. It inspires our spirits to realize that we can be delivered from evil and the evil one. It stimulates our souls and strengthens our resolve to be completely God's children. It is possible to sense the presence and power of Him who can save us from Satan and sin and our own selfish wills. We do not have to be enticed and trapped and tantalized by the enemy of our souls. We can be triumphant in temptation. To know this is to step out of despair into a delightful walk with our Father.

Our Master was not one to indulge in double-talk. He did not say one thing and mean another. He would not teach us to ask our heavenly Father for deliverance from evil if no deliverance was available. He would not instruct us to pray to be delivered from evil situations if our Father was unable to do so. But He *is*. And therein lies a great measure of the glory and joy of really knowing God as our Father.

Let us never, never forget that our Father does not want to see us succumb to temptation. He does not want to see us fall. He does not want to see us down in despair, struggling with self, and stained by sin. He wants us, as His maturing children, to grow up in strength so we can walk serenely with Him in the beauty of a strong, unsullied, intimate companionship.

Sometimes it helps us to understand temptation better if we look at it from our Father's viewpoint rather than ours. Our heavenly Father has precisely the same attitude to us, His children, as a concerned and intelligent human parent has toward his offspring. The concern and the love a good parent holds toward the child is expressed best by a deep desire to have the youngster mature and grow up into a strong, complete person with whom he can have rich rapport.

It is precisely the same with God and His children.

The human parent knows that a child does not grow up in one day. It is common knowledge that before we walk, we crawl. Before we run, we walk. Before we leap or jump, we run. It is a case of learning by degrees. Each stage is a testing, trying, tumbling time. Those of us who have raised children know full well some of the apprehension and dismay and also the joys of watching our young ones grow up.

And so it is with God our Father.

We have seen a wee one struggle to stand up on his own feet. The first few attempts he wobbles and weaves unsurely, inclined to fall to the floor. What does the parent do? He holds the little one's hand, steadies his shaky steps, leads him gently, encourages him to try again and again.

That is just what our Father in heaven does with us.

The little fellow falls flat on his face. He bumps his nose, bruises his head, blackens his eye. Does the parent beat him and berate him for his failure. No! Instead he sweeps him up in his arms, kisses away the tears, hugs him close, and dusts off his clothes.

This is the picture of our heavenly Father.

As the months roll by, and one year follows another, we see the child going on steadily from stage to stage. He walks. He runs. He leaps and jumps. He tackles hard hikes; he climbs high mountains, all with his parent's help, guidance, and encouragement. All the way, he is loved. He is given every assistance to keep on trying, to keep on improving, to keep on until he succeeds. And in every one of his triumphs, the parent shares a keen interest and joyous enthusiasm.

That is how it is in our walk with our heavenly Father.

To see ourselves in this way, endeavoring to mature spiritually, just as a child struggles to mature physically, is to see ourselves in a new light. Every tendency to fall, every temptation to go down, every struggle to stand or walk or leap are not testing situations which we meet alone. Our Father is right there. He is ever responsive, ready, eager, to extend His hand to help us the instant we need it.

Are we surprised then to have our Lord include this petition in His prayer? "Father, deliver us from evil!"

We need to remind ourselves, too, that no matter how often or hard we fall, He is there, waiting to pick us up and restore us. Why? Simply because we are His children, because He loves us, and because He knows that only as we go on do we grow up into His likeness.

Our struggles with sin and self and Satan, seen this way, are not the terrible trials we generally think them to be. Instead they are challenging, testing encounters that can strengthen our determination to go on with God. They inspire within us the resolve to mature into strong men and women with whom our heavenly Father loves to associate.

There are three definite, simple, and positive ways by which our heavenly Father delivers us from the evil one. The first of these has already been alluded to above. It is simply this: He is always there. He is always available. If we are His children, His gracious Spirit resides with us. And when we come into temptation, we need only remind ourselves that He is there and deliberately turn to Him.

It often helps to address Him aloud. Say something like this: "Oh Father, this is a bit beyond me. I can't cope with it. You can! Please extend Your hand, and, by Your Spirit, enable me to stand. Give me such a sense of Your presence by Your Spirit that I shall be empowered to walk through this situation without falling or stumbling."

The response of the Most High God to such a simple, sincere, and humble prayer suddenly provides tremendous strength to the tempted soul. One becomes acutely aware of Christ's presence by His Spirit. At that point the temptation loses its thrust. The impact of evil is dissipated, and an amazing sense of triumph sweeps into the soul. There is sublime power in the presence of God. In this way, God's children are reassured, and evil forces are routed.

The second means by which our heavenly Father delivers us from evil is really a very homespun, happy method. He endows us, by His Spirit, with spiritual common sense which He expects us to use in avoiding temptation. Paul tried to help young Timothy this way by writing to him and saying, "Flee these [evil] things" (1 Ti 6:11).

All of us know full well the areas of our lives where we are most liable to succumb to evil. We know those places and situations where we are most prone to fall for Satan's snares. We know the people that most readily influence us to do, say, or think evil. If we really want to be great, strong people for God it is utter folly and sheer stupidity to go to such places or to associate with such people. We have no right to expose ourselves unnecessarily to evil situations or wrong companions or wicked suggestions.

A child knows full well that he will fall if he plays on the slippery edge of a pond. No doubt, he has fallen there before. He has been warned of the danger by the parent. Still, he sometimes persists in playing there. Suddenly, he slips and falls down. The parent will pick him up again, but there will also be a sharp reprimand as well, with, perhaps, an even sharper smack on the seat. Why? Because the foolish youngster deliberately went into danger. The reprimand and discipline were administered in love and concern for his welfare. So it is with us and our Father. He expects us to use our God-given intelligence to keep out of trouble.

If we don't have enough spiritual fortitude to keep away from situations where we know we shall sin, then let us ask God to so invade us by His Spirit that we will. He has promised to give His Spirit to those who ask Him (Lk 11:11-13). The moment we do so in utter sincerity, we will find that He does in fact work in us, both to will and to do of His good pleasure (Phil 2:13). We will find that we do have the grit to get up and get out of evil situations.

At that point we shall find within ourselves both the desire and willingness to go where we should, do what we should, associate with whom we should, think as we should, and avoid what we should.

The Scriptures are replete with stirring accounts of men and women who positively refused to be caught in any compromising situation where they could be enticed by evil. They firmly determined that they would not, if they could help it, be in places or with people where they would be vulnerable to the evil one.

The third method of coping with evil that our heavenly Father has given us is the ability to battle it. There are bound to be times when we suddenly find ourselves struggling with Satan or sin or self, almost without warning. There is no way of anticipating the attack. There is no advance warning so that steps can be taken to avoid it. We find ourselves embroiled with evil, and the fight is fierce. What then?

Sometimes in these situations, we do not sense that

quiet, reassuring presence of our Father. It seems as though the very forces of evil surround us so that we are cut off from communication with God. And even when we do call upon Him, there appears to be no response, or, at least, so we imagine. Over and over, people protest that in such a crisis they feel completely overwhelmed and beaten down by the evil one.

Is there any strategy for routing Satan here? Is there anything available to God's child to launch a counterattack and frustrate the foe? Yes, there is.

In James 4:7 we are told very clearly, "Resist the devil, and he will flee from you." There is a sense in which God expects His children to be brave and bold in counterattacking Satan. Far, far too often we give ground to the enemy of our souls without any resistance. We simply slide into sinning without a struggle. This should not be.

The Spirit which God has given to us is not the spirit of fear, but rather, of power and of love and of a disciplined mind (2 Ti 1:7). We should not and need not feel apprehensive about resisting evil and the evil one. When we know full well what is right and proper and in accord with our Father's wishes, we need to be courageous enough to stand for it. And this we can do in the Spirit and by the strength of our Saviour, who Himself demonstrated that evil could be defeated. After all, Christ has vanquished the evil one. We need have no apologies for letting Satan know that we are aware of our powerful position and enormous resources within God's family.

It is worthy of note that whenever Christ was tempted or assailed by Satan, He immediately reacted by addressing Himself directly to His antagonist. With swift, stabbing strokes, using the Spirit's sword, God's Word,

He routed the wicked one. It was a demonstration of divine dilligence and spiritual stamina. Generally the encounter was over in a matter of a few brief moments after which Christ emerged triumphant.

If we wish to be armed against the evil one, we must equip ourselves with God's Word. Through reading it daily, thinking about it, and committing it to memory, we become fit to fight, just as our Lord did.

We live in an age when it is commonplace for many Christians to attribute many of their trials and troubles to the evil one. In part, this may be true. But as God's children we should give him less credence than many do. For, though he may be the ruler of this present evil world, though he may be the prince of the power of the air, though he may have cohorts of evil spirits at his command, he has no claim upon God's children, nor does he have the power to tempt or tantalize them, except by express permission from our Father in heaven. "We know [absolutely] that any one born of God does not [deliberately and knowingly] practice committing sin, but the One Who was begotten of God carefully watches over *and* protects him—Christ's divine presence within him preserves him against the evil—and the wicked one does not lay hold (get a grip) on him or touch [him]" (1 John 5:18, Amplified).

It is extremely important for us to understand this. It puts us into an enormously powerful stance. We see ourselves surrounded by the loving, eternal, constant protection of God Himself. We find we are within the great fraternity of God's family, where no assault can touch us, unless it is permitted within the providential purpose of our Father. And then it is allowed only for our own benefit.

The classic example of this truth is the life of Job. It was only by direct permission from God that Satan was allowed to tempt Job as he did. And without that permission he dared not touch either Job's family, his possessions, or his person. And after that dreadful ordeal was over, the end result for Job was enormous benefit and blessing.

Never, never forget that out of what seems to be evil, God our Father can and does bring great good to His children.

When we do encounter evil, we need not feel apprehensive. To the person walking with God his Father, there comes again and again the quiet assurance that all can be well. Our confidence lies, not in ourselves, nor in our ability to counteract evil, but rather in the character and strength of our Father who delivers us. He honors His own commitment to us as His children. He knows exactly why every evil assails us. And, bless His wondrous name, He can free us from it!

"Now unto him that is able to keep you from falling, and to present you faultless before the presence of his glory with exceeding joy, To the only wise God, our Saviour, be glory and majesty, dominion and power, both now and ever. Amen" (Jude 24-25).

TWELVE

For Thine Is the Kingdom, and the Power, and the Glory, for Ever. Amen

"For thine is the kingdom, and the power, and the glory for ever. Amen."

The benediction appears in only about half of the translations. It is, nevertheless, repeated in the prayer by most people. And because it serves as a beautiful benediction, it is included in this book.

But, over and beyond being a benediction, this part of the prayer is a powerful expression of praise to our Father in heaven. Just as the prayer opened in an attitude of reverence and honor, with the statement, "Hallowed be thy name," so now it closes with the reaffirmation of the greatness of our God. "Thine is the kingdom, and the power, and the glory for ever. Amen."

Do we really believe this?

Are we really sure the kingship of both heaven and earth is vested in our Father? Are we truly confident that He does control the events and destiny of all history? Do we see Him as the One who declares His Son to be King of kings and Lord of lords, before whom, one day, every human heart will bow in utter subjection?

"Wherefore, God also hath highly exalted him, and given him a name which is above every name: That at the name of Jesus every knee should bow, of things in heaven, and things in earth, and things under the earth: And that every tongue should confess that Jesus Christ is Lord, to the glory of God, the Father" (Phil 2:9-11).

Any less view of our Father in heaven is to see Him in a distorted manner. There must sweep over our souls a sense of awe and wonderment and exultation for the God of heaven. It is true, He is our Father; He is the loving One who draws us to Himself by His gracious Spirit with tenderness and compassion. But He is also the supreme Ruler of heaven and earth, before whom we must all one day stand to give account of ourselves. As such, He deserves our utmost respect.

Just as there is vested in Him all authority, so likewise there is vested in Him all power. Everything, and by that simple word *everything* is meant that all creation, be it in heaven or in earth, exists by virtue of His power.

> Now Christ is the visible expression of the invisible God. He existed before creation began, for it was through him that everything was made, whether spiritual or material, seen or unseen. Through him, and for him, also, were created power and dominion, ownership and authority. In fact, every single thing was created through, and for, him. He is both the first principle and the upholding principle of the whole scheme of creation. And now he is the head of the body which is the Church. Life from nothing began through him, and life from the dead began through him, and he is, therefore, justly called the Lord of all (Col 1:15-18, Phillips).

And again the serious, searching question we must ask ourselves is, Do I really believe this? Do I see my heavenly Father as absolute Sovereign of the universe? Do I recognize Him as the ultimate power behind the scenes, who dictates and determines the whole course of history? Do I comprehend, even feebly, that everything that exists does so by virtue of His express permission and ordained will?

If I do, then there is bound to be within my spirit an overwhelming respect for Him. There will steal over my spirit a reverence of profound proportions. And this great regard for my God will color and condition all of my thoughts, actions, attitudes, and motives.

No longer will it be good enough for me to assume rather naively that God my Father is some remote Deity hovering on the periphery of this planet's little stage, a rather benevolent Being somewhere "out there," who can be appealed to in a crisis. Instead, I shall see Him as the central Figure in the whole drama of the universe. I shall see Him as the key Character by whose word the whole world scene can change. I shall see Him as the One who, because of His power, determines the destiny of both men and nations, yes, and much more than this, the Director of the entire universe, both natural and supernatural.

Is it not appropriate then, and very proper, that this prayer, taught us by our Lord, should terminate on a rising theme of exultation and praise? Who else is so truly deserving of our adulation? Who else so merits our most devoted and genuine exaltation?

For most of us, our God is far, far too feeble. Our mental and spiritual pictures of Him, projected before us by our own weak and inadequate concepts of His character, are but caricatures of His true Person. We simply do not see our Father all resplendent in His majesty and power and glory. Few of us have more than a flickering comprehension of His might. At our best we seem to catch only fleeting, passing glimpses of His true greatness.

A few select, and it seems widely separated, human beings have been afforded the great honor to have an intimate view of God. Their reaction has always been the same. They are totally overwhelmed by the utter majesty, the indescribable magnitude, the awesome glory of His Person. Their immediate impulse is to bow low in humble obeisance, to worship, to break out in spontaneous praise and adoration.

It is therefore not the least surprising that Jesus Christ, who, more than any mortal man, knew His Father intimately, would instruct us to ascribe to Him these honors. To do less would be to leave the prayer incomplete.

I say this in great earnestness just here. We are often so preoccupied with our petitions to our Father that we completely forget to praise Him for who He is and what He has done. If we are to have a balanced, wholesome relationship to God, it is imperative that we not only come to Him freely with our petitions but also reverently with our praise and gratitude.

All through the Scriptures, God's people are encouraged to honor, respect, and praise Him. Praise is just as important to God as prayer is to the well-being of humans. I bless God in rendering to Him my reverent praise and genuine gratitude for being who He is. He in turn blesses me by responding to and respecting my prayers and petitions. In essence, such communion between God and man becomes an intimate exchange of enormous benefit to both.

We seldom realize how much we impoverish our own souls and deprive our Father in heaven of deep delight by neglecting to praise Him. Not only does He deserve

our praise, He also expects it. Our Lord made this abundantly clear at the time of His triumphal entry into
Jerusalem. Some of the Pharisees felt the shouts of
praise and cries of approbation given to Christ by the
crowds as He rode into the great city were quite out of
order. His immediate response was that if the people did
not praise Him, then the very stones would shout His
praises (Lk 19:28-40).

There is inherent in the very character of God such
splendor, glory, greatness, justice, love, generosity, that
it demands our deepest adoration and gratitude. It is
only when we grasp something of His glorious goodness, greatness, graciousness, generosity in dealing
with us as His children, that there begins to spring up
from our innermost spirits a clear flowing stream of
praise and gratitude to Him. This is the great, great
secret to a sublime communion with Him. It is the key to
keen, zestful relationship with our heavenly Father.

The interrelationship between me and my heavenly
Father finds a parallel in the interaction between a
human parent and a child. When a child comes softly
and sincerely to a parent, with endearing expressions of
gratitude and appreciation for what the parent is or has
done, it unlocks that parent's heart in a wondrous way.
The parent's spirit is deeply stirred and moved and
melted by the child's expression of gratitude, love, and
appreciation. The net result is that the parent now, more
than ever, is disposed to lavish even more love and care
and benefits on the youngster. This is out of gratitude
for the praise and appreciation bestowed by the child.
So there is set up between child and parent a two-way
communication of blessing upon blessing, benefit upon
benefit.

This is precisely the relationship which our Father in

heaven longs to have with us. After all, the very under-
lying reason for His making men and women at all was
to have sons and daughters with whom He could have
intimate communion. It was His longing, in love, for
such a relationship that prompted Him to produce a
plan of redemption and reconciliation for His wayward
children. He desires above all else to have us come into
that simple, yet exquisite family relationship with Him,
where He can bless us and we can be a blessing to Him.
He has endured enormous anguish and suffering to
make this possible. But its greatest compensation for
Him lies in the praise and love and gratitude of His
people. He looks on the travail of His soul and is satisfied because He has brought sons from out the human
race to glory. He has found those whom He could transform into His own likeness and character. Therein lies
His joy.

Our Lord had all of this clearly in His mind when He
concludes on the theme, "For thine is the glory for
ever."

As has been pointed out previously in this book,
God's great glory is His impeccable character, and His
splendid, sublime character is His glory! Nothing we
mere mortals know among men can in any way be even
remotely compared to the character and person of our
Father in heaven. Yet, wonder upon wonders, He deigns
to stoop down and impart a portion of that glory to an
earnest, searching, seeking soul who longs for His true
likeness.

That great poet, David, gives poignant expression to
this inner heart yearning, in Psalm 17:15, when he says,
"As for me, I will behold thy face in righteousness; I
shall be satisfied, when I awake, with thy likeness."

Paul, the grand apostle, put it this way: "But we all,

with open face beholding as in a glass the glory of the Lord, are changed into the same image from glory to glory, even as by the Spirit of the Lord" (2 Co 3:18).

There it is. All the glory, all the grandeur, all the greatness of God's character stands vested in our Father forever and forever. Yet through and by the magnanimous generosity of His own self, He gladly, willingly, eagerly imparts it to us by His gracious Spirit. Every good thing we do, every noble impulse we own, every generous thought we think, every praise-worthy attribute we possess, has as its source and fountain the character and Person of our Father in heaven.

Are we surprised, then, that our Lord should end the prayer on this point? He says, "For ever!" It has always been that way. It always will be. God being God, there is neither beginning nor end to the benefits our Father bestows upon His children. They are new every day. They come without interruption or intermission. They come from the inexhaustible supply of His own being. What an assurance, what a consolation, what a strength to those of us, who, in simple, yet sincere and implicit trust, have put our complete confidence in Him.

It is no wonder the psalmist shouts out across the long centuries of time, "This is the day the LORD hath made; we will rejoice and be glad in it" (Ps 118:24).

Today, tomorrow, and every day given to us is a day direct from the hand of our Father. It is a day in which we can fully appreciate all the advantages and benefits He brings to us as His children. It is a day during which we can turn our hearts and minds back toward Him in sincere gratitude and praise. And out of this there flows between us that serene sense of oneness which is so very precious to God's people.

There are some who attempt to live their Christian

lives out of a sense of duty to God. It cannot be done. It becomes a dreadful burden and bondage. There are others who endeavor to maintain their relationship to God by ritual and routine. This degenerates to awful boredom. Still others hope to live in spiritual communion with God by indulging in emotional, ecstatic experiences. These are delusive and temporary. A few struggle resolutely to live stoicly with great self-discipline and inner determination of spirit. They grow weary in their well-doing.

But for the soul who understands something of the wondrous goodness of his Father in heaven, who feels his heart warmed with genuine gratitude for the generosity of God, who feels appreciation and love welling up within because of his Father's love, such a soul has found the secret to a serene and enduring relationship with his God. This is forever, unchanging, undiminished!

Such a person discovers that the motivation, the drives, the desires which now determine his relationship to God and others, are not those of his or her own making. They have their origin with God. Their source is the Person of God Himself. In other words, we love because He first loved us.

Our lives, our prayers, our praise, are all bound up in an attitude of gratitude to God our Father. This was the way our Lord lived. In everything, He sensed and knew that His part was to give thanks, even for the cup which spoke of His blood to be shed for us and the bread which spoke of His body to be broken for us. If this then was the attitude of gratitude motivating the very life of our Lord, God's own Son, who taught us this prayer, surely how much more it should be ours!

Only in this way can we live lives that will reflect,

even if only feebly, the glory and character of our Father in heaven. These are the lives that will bless Him and benefit others around us. Amen. "So let it be."

"Yes, Father, may all the petitions and all the praise bound up in this brief yet wondrous prayer become a vital part of our very makeup. Grant it, O God, for Your dear name's sake, as well as ours."

"Amen."